H-14

Biking Northern Michigan

The Best & Safest Routes
in the Northern Lower Peninsula

Robert Downes

The Wandering

PRESS

Traverse City, Michigan

Published by
The Wandering Press
Traverse City, Michigan

Cataloguing-in Publication Data pending
from the Library of Congress

ISBN 978-0-9904670-0-7

Printed in the United States of America

Biking In Northern Michigan is available at a discount
when purchased in bulk for educational & fundraising use or by organizations.
For details, email bob@planetbackpacker.net

www.planetbackpacker.net

On the cover: Riding the North Eastern State Trail from Alpena to Cheboygan.

South Africa - 2009

For George Foster

Also by Robert Downes

Planet Backpacker

Travels With My Wife

My Thanks

Some of the routes in this book were pioneered in the company of old cycling buddies from way back -- Troy Mariage, Adair Correll, Ron Klinefelter, Mark Doherty, Bill Brundage, Garry Demarest, Jim Mudgett, the docs from Munson Medical Center and many others who suffered my company or allowed me to tag along on long rides out of Traverse City.

Special thanks to Michigan's Center for Shared Solutions and Department of Technology, Management & Budget for granting permission to use the public domain maps which served as the basis for my renditions. Without their kind permission there would simply be no book.

Thanks also to Tim Brick of Brick Wheels and Bob McLain of McLain Cycle, respectively, who sold me many fine bicycles through the years, and to their staffs for their fine service and repairs. And to the staff at Latitude 45 in Petoskey for fixing my bike on a moment's notice and offering advice on the routes around Walloon Lake and Lake Charlevoix.

Thanks to the good people at TART Trails, the Top of Michigan Trails Council, Vasa Trails, Sleeping Bear National Lakeshore and the Cherry Capital Cycling Club for doing so much to make Northern Michigan a bicycling paradise beyond compare.

Thanks to my wife, Jeannette Wildman, who has been a stalwart companion on many miles shared together, both on day rides and week-long adventures.

Thanks finally to my best friend and business partner George Foster, to whom this book is dedicated, for giving me the freedom and the opportunity to travel, write and succeed far beyond what I ever imagined in my youthful dreams.

Contents

Introduction

I was riding along in a cold, gray curtain of early morning rain when a huge bear crashed out of the forest and wandered into the road not 30 yards ahead of me.

I'd been pedaling for two days in a steady rain and had spent the night camping under the eaves of a park restroom, drying my soggy clothes under its hand dryer. Yet here it was, 7 in the morning and I was soaked to the bone again with a bear gaping at me in mutual surprise.

I rummaged for the camera in my frontpack, desperate to snap the photo of a lifetime. But before I could hit the shutter, the bear plunged into the underbrush at the side of the road. A shower of raindrops exploded from his glistening fur as he melted into the brush.

That was in the rainforest beyond the Alps of Vancouver Island and not Northern Michigan, but I've been searching for that bear's distant cousin ever since, especially along the back roads of Benzie County or on the forest trails heading north to the Mackinac Straits. Someday, perhaps...

Since that 800-mile bicycle camping trip around the Pacific Northwest 25 years ago, I've cycled many thousands of miles along the roads and bike paths of Northern Michigan, not always looking for a bear, but ready with a camera if one does decide to show up.

Some of the routes in this book date back to my days as a triathlete hammering out 50, 75 or 100-mile rides each weekend in the '80s and '90s. In recent years, I've ridden for fitness and fun, and to explore the long forest routes to the Mackinac Straits.

I've also had the pleasure of cycling in Australia, Costa Rica, Nicaragua, South Africa, Ireland, England, Tuscany, Croatia, Vietnam, China, India, Sri Lanka and more than 1,000 miles across continental Europe.

Based on that experience, nothing compares to Northern Michigan when it comes to being one of the finest cycling regions on earth. We've got it all: a network of more than 1,000 miles of bike routes, lovely small towns reached by quiet roads, hundreds of lakes, vast forests, and "the most beautiful place in America" with the cycle-friendly Sleeping Bear National Lakeshore.

ONE OF THE BEST

Michigan arguably holds the title of America's "Trail State."

Consider that Michigan is second in the nation when it comes to rail-trail conversions with 109 trails. Only Pennsylvania outdoes us with 113 trails.

Michigan is also second in the nation with 1,311 rail-trail conversion miles. Only Wisconsin does better with 1,394 trail miles.

Additionally, Michigan one of only two states in the nation which has legislated a mandatory minimum of funding for non-motorized transportation, the other state being Oregon.

Add to that, most cyclists in the state would likely agree that the very best-of-the-best routes are in the region known as Northern Michigan.

WHERE WE'RE AT

"Northern Michigan" refers to the *northern Lower Peninsula* and not the Upper Peninsula, which is geographically and culturally distinct from the rest of the state. In the 1970s, separatists advocated having the U.P. declared the 51st state, Superior. Undoubtably there's good cycling up that way, but the U.P. is better known for its backpacking, camping, hunting and fishing opportunities.

Down here "below the Bridge," Northern Michigan has topped many national "best" lists in recent years for its scenery, cuisine, lifestyle, recreation, and of course, cycling.

In fact, many tourists will tell you that their favorite experience while visiting Northern Michigan was the simple joy of riding the bike paths in and around Traverse City, Petoskey and the Sleeping Bear National Lakeshore. We natives can tell who these riders are by the broad grins on their faces, having the time of their lives.

STAYING SAFE

As a writer and a cyclist, one of my overriding concerns (no pun intended), is safety. Dozens of times through the years I've been buzzed far out in the middle of nowhere by yahoos in pickup trucks who have plenty of road to steer clear, but opt for coming within a finger's length of my bike. Oh, you too?

I never know if it's stupidity or murderous intent at work with these drivers. But considering that the hazards of cycling have increased tenfold as a result of drivers texting, talking on the phone, and even watching films while driving, I've grown more cautious through the years. Unfortunately, you'll also find drinkers and druggers on the roads of Northern Michigan and confused old folks who can't quite see where they're going.

Traverse City in 2013 was a case in point. Numerous riders were struck by cars last year, including some friends who now suffer life-long injuries.

Local newspapers were filled with accusatory letters from cyclists vs. drivers, casting blame on each others' bad habits. In early July, the inherent hazards of cycling were framed in the starkest possible terms by the death of Kelly Boyce-Hurlbert, who was struck by a car and dragged 150 feet while biking home from her job after midnight. Her killer was never found despite the investigation of hundreds of tips provided to city detectives and the FBI. Hundreds of cyclists rode through town in her memorial service.

Consider that 726 cyclists were killed in 2012 by motorists. That's more than 10 times the number of Americans who were killed in Mexico that year -- a place many now fear to visit due to its drug gang violence verging on a civil war. Ironically, you might think twice about vacationing in Mexico, without giving a thought to your safety on the much meaner streets of the U.S.A.

So when possible, I've advocated routes that include bike paths or lanes. That's not possible on some popular routes, such as around most of Old Mission Peninsula or Leelanau County, but in those cases, this guide offers advice on safety measures.

A STARTING POINT

I can't claim that *Biking Northern Michigan* is an all-inclusive guide to the region; there are many worthy routes which have been omitted by dint of the vast number of cycling options. One could, for instance, spend an entire summer of weekends exploring the routes around Leelanau County alone. I've also excluded some notable race routes which are great rides, but essentially "go nowhere."

Rather, consider this book a starting point for your own exploration of Northern Michigan. The maps within will help you plan your own adventures.

My hope is that you'll use this guide to explore hundreds of miles of bike routes -- enough to keep you pedaling for years on end -- all while arriving safely at home in top shape with pleasant memories.

See you out there... and if you spot a bear in your travels (or his little brother Boo-Boo in the text), feel free to drop me a line -- bob@planetbackpacker.net

TC's Hagerty team at the Cherry Roubaix.

Essential Gear

The bicycle is a relatively fragile beast, and even experienced riders tend to forget this until they're miles from home without a spare tire, a patch kit or even a pump.

Many of us depend on the kindness of strangers when we have a breakdown. This can be an iffy proposition, and at the very least an inconvenience for those hailed to help you change your tire.

Broken chains, numerous flats, expired tire kits, broken pumps, sidewall blow-outs... these are some of the problems I've encountered to my dismay through the years, followed by long walks.

It's far better to be capable of self-rescue. Bonus: you'll be a hero to those unprepared cycle buddies of yours when they're in a jam. Here's what I carry on every ride longer than 10 miles:

Tools & Supplies

• Fluorescent vest or jersey for maximum visibility
• Mobile phone
• Spare tire (2 if on a ride of 50+ miles).
• Fresh patch kit & tire spoons -- change yearly, since the glue in these kits tend to dry up.
• Bike pump -- check each spring to see if the gasket still works.
• All-purpose tool, such as The Alien.
• A 3x4" piece of cardboard for use repairing a sidewall blow-out.
• Spare chain link.
• A pair of cheap rubber water shoes -- so you don't have to walk for miles in your cleats if your bike is totally bollixed.
• A bungee cord -- use it to wrap your rubber shoes around the seat post of your bike.
• A bandanna -- to cover your face in dusty or buggy situations, or for wiping your hands after fixing a chain or a flat
• A back-up plan. Say you bent a rim beyond repair and you're w-a-y out yonder. Who you gonna call?

First Aid:

Ever swallowed a bee while riding? It ain't pretty. Here's what I pack on even short rides:

• Mitagator sting & bite treatment scrub: Concocted of ground walnut paste and Sodium Bicarbonate, this salve is worth its weight in gold when you get stung. It leaches the stinging poison from your flesh.
• Benadryl tabs -- if you swallow a stinging insect and get nailed in the throat, this or a similar antihistamine can help keep you breathing.
• Bandaids -- for those times when you forget to cross the railway tracks at a 90-degree angle.
• Sunscreen & lip balm -- especially for those long rides without cover.

Safety Stuff

Did you know that it's illegal to text while riding a bicycle in Michigan? Or that it's illegal to talk on a mobile phone while riding a bike if it keeps you from having both hands on your handlebars?

This is from the Michigan Vehicle Code as it pertains to cyclists.

In light of numerous car-bicycle accidents, the rules & regs of Michigan law have been widely distributed by the League of Michigan Cyclists and other bicycling groups across the state.

Most of these laws involve common sense safety measures, such as the following:

- It's illegal to ride more than two abreast.
- You're required to have a headlight on your bike which can be seen 500 feet away if you're riding after dark. Your rear reflector must be visible at least 100 feet away by a driver traveling with the low-beams on his or her vehicle.
- Bicycles must be equipped with a brake.
- Bicyclists are required by law to signal their turns.

Some of these laws go unheeded by cyclists, giving rise to accidents.

Interesting to note, under the MVC, it *is* legal to ride on sidewalks under some circumstances, provided you give pedestrians the right-of-way and there are no local ordinances against it (as is the case in downtown Traverse City). Also, under state law, you can't be charged with a DUI while riding a bicycle, although "other ordinances may apply... such as being intoxicated and a danger to oneself or another."

Need more legal stuff? Check out the link at http://www.lmb.org . Otherwise, here are some safety tips from the files of yours truly, garnered through years of hard experience:

- **Don't ride to exhaustion:** On most of the occasions that I've fallen off a bicycle, it's been the result of pounding out too many miles, sometimes in faster, stronger company with too little water or food for replenishment. Exhaustion can literally 'trip you up' or cause you to do dumb things, like roll through stop signs. Generally, you'll fall while stopping -- when you least expect it -- as the result of being suddenly dizzy and disoriented.

Get off your bike and walk a couple hundred yards when you're pooped. It will clear your head and refresh your legs.

• **Stay hydrated:** This goes hand-in-hand with the perils of exhaustion since dehydrated muscles are tired muscles. Keep lubricated and you'll be lot sharper in the saddle.

• **When in doubt, wait it out:** A few years ago, a fixed-gear racer took a chance on flying through an intersection on busy Division Street in Traverse City and suffered a broken limb for his indiscretion.

Never take a chance at an intersection. You may not see a motorcycle speeding your way, or may misjudge how fast a motorist is coming. And if ever there's a time when your chain is going to slip off the cogs, it's when you're jamming it hard to get ahead of traffic veering down on you at 45mph.

Also, be aware that riding in town is generally far more hazardous than rolling through open countryside for the simple fact that your chances of a collision are multiplied many times over by the abundance of intersections. Wait and observe.

• **Clothing matters:** If you're wearing dark colors, you might as well be dressed in camouflage. Cyclists wearing some variant of black or brown blend in with the trees directly ahead of a motorist and may be hard to spot. This is especially true if a driver is fiddling with a mobile phone or distracted by kids or the radio.

It's far better to wear a fluorescent jersey or jacket, not only because a motorist can easily spot you from 500 feet away, but also because of the underlying message that fluorescent apparel provides. Fluorescent vests and blaze orange are worn by road crews, utility workers, tree cutters and hunters -- they signal caution, respect, the law. A yahoo bearing down on you in his high-riding Silverado on swamp hawg tires is likely to give you a little more berth if he sees you wearing the same colors as 'his' tribe.

• **Don't ride drunk.** You'd think this would be self-evident, but given the popularity of bike pub crawls, it's worth noting that your balance on a bicycle is seriously affected after a drink or three.

• **The helmet thing...** These days when you see a cyclist riding without a helmet it's generally because he or she is inexperienced and rarely rides a bicycle except when on vacation every couple of years 'Up North.'

Some inexperienced riders don't wear helmets because they don't wish to bear the expense of coughing up $35 or so for a piece of equipment they don't plan to use very often. Others think helmets are 'sissy' or mess with their hair.

You're not required by law to wear a helmet, but if you don't care for your own safety, at least have some consideration for the loved-ones in your family who'll be wiping your ass or changing your catheter for years on end if you take a crack on the noggin that's beyond repair.

• **Bee safe:** Do you fear rattlesnakes, grizzly bears and sharks? Forget about it; bees and wasps account for the highest number of deaths from the animal kingdom each year in the U.S. -- 53 on the average.

That's a small number compared to the 726 bicyclists who were killed by motorists in 2012, but fatal or not, bee and wasp stings seem to be fairly common while cycling. As mentioned in the "Essential Gear" section, a couple tabs of Benadryl and some Mitagator scrub in your first aid kit can help alleviate the misery of a sting.

• **Railway crossings:** Crossing tracks at an angle of 45 degrees or so is a common mistake by many inexperienced cyclists. Crossing tracks at a sharp angle traps the front wheel of your bike with predictable results. The only safe way to cross a set of tracks is straight on at a perpendicular, 90 degree angle: +

Notes:

Grand Traverse

Most of the cycling opportunities in Grand Traverse County run to the north, with Traverse City serving as a launching pad for the Leelanau Trail, Old Mission Peninsula, and within the city itself.

You won't lack for camaraderie with fellow cyclists in Traverse City; with seven bicycle stores in town and various racing teams and clubs, TC is the gold standard for cycling in Michigan. Check out the Cherry Roubaix cycle races in town on the third weekend of August, or the numerous tours in summer and hordes of riders every night after work and you're likely to become a believer.

Don't Miss:

- The TART Trail System
- Boardman Lake Trail
- Old Mission Peninsula
- Kalkaska to TC
- The Leelanau Trail

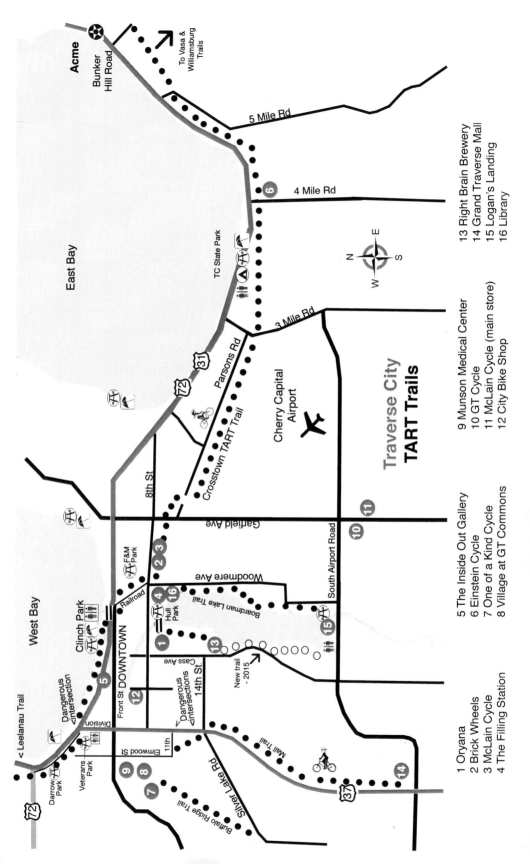

Traverse City
TART Trails

Acme

East Bay

West Bay

< Leelanau Trail

To Vasa & Williamsburg Trails

5 Mile Rd

4 Mile Rd

3 Mile Rd

Bunker Hill Road

TC State Park

Parsons Rd

Crosstown TART Trail

8th St

Garfield Ave

Cherry Capital Airport

South Airport Road

Woodmere Ave

Boardman Lake Trail

New trail - 2015

Cass Ave

14th St.

Dangerous intersections

11th

Elmwood St

Silver Lake Rd

Buffalo Ridge Trail

Mall Trail

DOWNTOWN

Front St

Railroad

Clinch Park

Dangerous intersection

Division

Veterans Park

Darrow Park

F&M Park

Hull Park

1 Oryana
2 Brick Wheels
3 McLain Cycle
4 The Filling Station

5 The Inside Out Gallery
6 Einstein Cycle
7 One of a Kind Cycle
8 Village at GT Commons

9 Munson Medical Center
10 GT Cycle
11 McLain Cycle (main store)
12 City Bike Shop

13 Right Brain Brewery
14 Grand Traverse Mall
15 Logan's Landing
16 Library

Traverse City's TART Trail

Distance: 10.5 from end-to-end.
Bike recommendation: All good; use mountain bikes on the Vasa Trail
Essentials: Beware of weaving toddlers
Traffic: None
Difficulty: Easy does it

One of the first things visitors notice when they roll into Traverse City is the scores of walkers, runners and cyclists enjoying the TART Trail along West Grand Traverse Bay.

Traverse City (or TC) has been the region's epicenter for the fitness and recreation lifestyle since at least the 1970s, so the bike path movement which blossomed in the '80s was a natural fit.

The trail running along West Bay and Clinch Park Beach dates back more than 30 years. In 1998, four local trail groups got together to form Traverse Area Recreation and Transportation Trails, Inc. Today, TART has five paid staffers and a board of 14 volunteers. You can meet some of them if you ride the annual Tour de TART fundraiser to Suttons Bay in late July.

Since the late '90s, a network of trails have been established in all directions throughout TC and beyond, with plans for more in the near future.

Need a bike? You can rent one at Brick Wheels or McLain Cycle on 8th Street, right on the bike path, or at the kiosk at Clinch Park Beach.

THE TRAILS

Officially, there are 8 trails in the TART system, but some are combined with others. Here's the lowdown:

• **The Crosstown TART Trail:** This 10.5-mile trail runs from Greilickville on the west side of TC, past downtown and out along East Bay to Acme. The trail is popular with commuters, families and locals getting their exercise after work.

A good place to start is at the Open Space at the foot of Union Street downtown. If you need a bike, you can rent one near the new pavilion at Clinch Park, which also offers kayaks and stand-up paddle boards.

Carry on under a bridge across the Boardman River and through a residential area and you'll soon come to **Brick Wheels** and **McLain Cycle.** Respective owners Tim Brick and Bob McLain are the original titans of cycling in TC and have thrown their support behind local trails, races and other cycling events for over 30 years. Well worth a stop.

Heading east across busy Garfield Road for two miles, you'll also come across **Einstein Cycle** at 4 Mile Road, a shop which specializes in the needs of racers.

The path passes Traverse City State Park and along East Bay, with the paved portion ending at Bunker Hill Road.

An obscure route takes you up Bunker Hill Road past the turnoff to the Vasa Trailhead to Lautner Road, where a paved bike path picks up again, running to M-72 in Williamsburg. This portion of the trail ends in the middle of nowhere and is useful primarily for cycling on via the roadways to Elk Rapids. In any case, beware of the crumbling, narrow stretch of Bunker Hill Road, as the afternoon sun is directly in the eyes of motorists in the summer.

Be aware of the many family groups along the TART Trail, who tend to be inexperienced when it comes to cycling etiquette. Their wee ones typically weave into the path of oncoming cyclists. If you see a toddler on training wheels, take your speed down a notch.

• **The Leelanau Trail:** Running 17 miles from Greilickville to Suttons Bay, this trail is the top bike path out of TC. See the section on page 35 for details.

• **The Boardman Lake Trail:** This lovely 2-mile trail travels along the heavily-wooded east side of Boardman Lake, just south of downtown.

The trail starts at Hull Park near the **Traverse Area District Library** (worth a stop). It's paved most of the way, but includes a crushed limestone stretch near the south end of the lake at Airport Road.

On the way back you'll want to stop at **The Filling Station** near

The memorial ride for Kelly Boyce-Hurlbert drew hundreds of cyclists.

Hull Park. This is TC's former railroad station which has been converted into a brewpub serving artisan pizzas and salad. Also at the depot is the **Cycle Pub**, a 14-passenger trolley which excited patrons pedal around town to various drinking establishments. GLBT-oriented cyclists will be cheered to find the **Sidetraxx Bar** just a stone's throw to the west -- it's considered one of TC's hottest dance scenes.

Continue west past a sailing school and bridge over the Boardman River where you'll often find a mob of teenagers risking their necks with high-flying plunges into the water. Up the hill is the **Oryana Food Co-op**, which is *the* place to be for anyone interested in whole foods. The co-op includes an organic cafe and coffeeshop, often with local musicians performing.

Plans are in the works to pave a new link of the pathway to

The spring Tweed Ride at the Grand Traverse Commons.

14th Street in 2014, just a few blocks south of Oryana. Push on to 16th Street and you'll find the sprawling **Right Brain Brewery**, a popular spot with locals.

Eventually, TART hopes to circle the entire lake once some easement issues are resolved along busy Airport Road.

Worth noting: The brushy area around Boardman Lake, particularly southeast of Oryana, has been TC's hobo jungle since at least the 1930s. Most of the homeless people you'll see along the trail and at Hull Park are harmless victims of substance abuse and mental illness who are trying hard not to be noticed. But on occasion there can be some rough-looking characters to steer clear of and there was an attempted abduction of a woman on the Boardman Lake Trail near S. Airport Road in 2013. If this makes you nervous, cycle with a friend, or ride the trail after 5 p.m. when many locals are out getting their exercise.

• **Buffalo Ridge Trail:** This is the newest trail in the system on the west side of town, running from the Grand Traverse Commons uphill to Copper Ridge on Silver Lake Road.

The trail passes the Commons' **Community Gardens** tended by locals, with a new **Botanical Gardens** project underway as well as the **Historic Barns** cultural center.

The trail is worth investigating because of its proximity to the

Village at the Grand Traverse Commons, a former mental hospital built in 1885 which is now one of the biggest renovation projects in the United States.

Founded by James Decker Munson, M.D., the former Northern Michigan Asylum housed thousands of mentally-ill and depressed patients for a century after it was built. Dr. Munson eschewed restraints whenever possible in favor of manual labor and exercise as therapy.

Thus, hundreds of acres were under cultivation just south of the hospital in addition to a prize-winning herd of milk cows. One cow, T. Colantha Walker, held the record as the top milk-producing bovine in the world. You can still see her tombstone near the Historic Barns just off the bike path.

The Village, housed in the former Building 50, constitutes a second mini-downtown for the area, with shops and restaurants lining its Mercado corridor. Nearby is the **Left Foot Charley winery, Pleasanton Bakery, Underground Cheesecake** and other worthy stops.

Also worth noting, many mountain bike enthusiasts enjoy riding the rugged, unpaved trails in the hills just west of the Commons. The new **One of a Kind Cycle** shop is right at the trailhead, which is also popular with snowshoers in the winter.

For the future, the Buffalo Ridge Trail will be extended another 4 miles through the suburbs south and west of TC, including to a new **YMCA** fitness center and Olympic swimming pool.

The Vasa Pathway: For mountain bikes only, this sandy trail through the Pere Marquette Forest was originally established for cross-country skiers, who are still the primary users.

The trail hosts the annual Vasa National Ski Race in February with distances of 27 and 50k. A section is also included as part of the Iceman Cometh mountain bike race, which draws more than 5,000 riders in November. (See Kalkaska to Traverse City, page 29.)

The trail is also popular with fat bike riders in all seasons, although they are an irritation to many XC skiers in the winter.

Exclusively for mountain bikers is the **Vasa Singletrack**, a 12-mile loop off Supply Road. Riding in a counter-clockwise direction is mandatory; otherwise you'll likely to bang heads with hard-charging mountain bike racers in training.

• **The Mall Trail:** Ironically, one of the least-used trails in Traverse City is also one of the oldest. The Mall Trail was built in 1997, running from 14th Street along busy U.S. 31 for 2 miles to Airport Road and the **Grand Traverse Mall.**

It's a long uphill climb the whole way with the roar of traffic in your ears. Take care at the fast food driveways that you don't get clobbered by inattentive motorists -- this is 'their' turf, after all. The trail is used primarily by commuters working at the many chain stores along the route.

HAZARDS

There are three hazardous intersections of note in Traverse City -- all off Division Street (US 31):

• The TART Trail crossing at Division and West Bayshore Drive is especially dangerous. Drivers turning right off Division are infamous for their disregard of cyclists and pedestrians who are crossing the street from the bay.

• 14th Street at Division. If you're taking the Mall Trail, you'll want to be a wary of this hectic crossroads.

• 11th Street at Division. Many cyclists attempt this busy intersection to reach the Grand Traverse Commons. Forget about it; either cross at the light at 7th Street or a block down at 10th where there tends to be a natural break in oncoming traffic.

LOOKING AHEAD

For the future, TART is investigating the possibility of a new **Boardman River Trail** which will run 24 miles from TC to the North Country Trail near the burg of Mayfield along existing dirt paths and two-tracks. After reaching the North Country Trail, mountain bikers will be able to head back via the Vasa Trail for a 46-mile circuit.

TART is also considering the creation of a new 50-mile trail which would run from TC through Elk Rapids to Charlevoix. Someday, cyclists may be able to ride off-road all the way from TC to Mackinaw City, a distance of 106 miles.

Web: http://traversetrails.org

The Jolly Pumpkin Ride held in May.

Old Mission Peninsula

Distance: 20, 39 & 40 miles
Bike recommendation: Road bike or hybrid
Essentials: Sunscreen, tool & tire kit, fluorescent jersey, water
Traffic: Medium
Difficulty: Easy to semi-tough, depending on length

The Old Mission Peninsula has been the top road-biking route out of Traverse City for decades. You'll find cyclists here at all hours of the day and some of those zipping past you are likely to be among the best cycle racers in the state.

The pleasures of the peninsula are especially apparent along East Grand Traverse Bay. If you're gung-ho enough to rise at 5 a.m. on a summers' day, you'll be rewarded with a glorious sunrise and the blissful sensation of feeling in sync with the universe.

The peninsula divides East and West Grand Traverse Bays and runs 19 miles to a small park with a lighthouse at the tip. You don't have to ride the whole circuit, however; there are several cross-overs from one side of the peninsula to the other for those preferring shorter routes.

Quiet roads run down the east side and middle of the peninsula, with traffic picking up considerably on narrow Peninsula Drive on the west side. Fortunately, most commuters tend to favor speeding

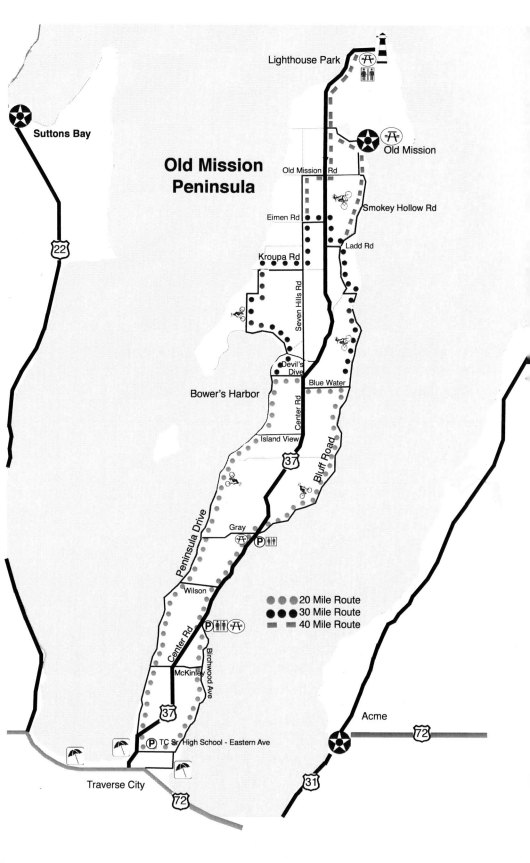

down the aptly-named Center Road which forms a spine down the middle. Even Center Road isn't a bad ride though, since it includes a wide bike path shoulder on either side all the way out to the vineyards.

THE OPTIONS

Following are a few of the best routes. Park at Traverse City Senior High School on Eastern Avenue at the foot of the peninsula and head east for all of the following rides.

Note: if you wish to skip residential Birchwood Ave. and Center Road entirely, drive about 5 miles out Center and cycle from the roadside park just before Bluff and Gray roads.

• **15 miles:** This route takes you to a point with a beautiful view of East Bay on Bluff Road. Ride north on Birchwood to Center Road. About 6 miles from town you turn right off Center onto Bluff Road and carry on round a long sweeping curve to the point where the road heads north again. Look familiar? This vista is where many automobile commercials have been shot over the years. You can ride back the way you came, or head over the hill (a big one) on Gray Road and ride back down Peninsula Drive on the west side.

• **20 miles:** Follow the same route (above) to Bluff Road and keep going about 3 miles to Blue Water Road. Turning left, you'll be rewarded with a stout hill climb past some orchards to Center Road. Head north a short distance to Seven Hills Road and take a left on Devil's Dive. From there it's back down Peninsula Drive to home.

• **30 miles:** This route takes you several miles past Blue Water Road to where it curves around to Smokey Hollow Road and a challenging hill. At the top you roll through an orchard to Ladd Road (left). Then it's right on Center to Eimen Road (left), until you hit Seven Hills Road (left). After a few miles you head right on Peninsula Drive or Bowers Harbor Road to head back into town along the West Bay shoreline.

• **40 miles:** This route takes you past Ladd Road down a steep hill to the Village of Old Mission. From there, the route winds back to Center Road for a run of several miles to Old Mission State Park and its lighthouse. Most riders cut west on the way back to head down the roller-coaster of Seven Hills Road and Peninsula Drive.

A LITTLE HISTORY

Old Mission was the first white settlement in the Traverse City area, with Presbyterian missionaries Rev. Peter Dougherty and Rev. John Fleming arriving at the present-day site of Old Mission Harbor from Mackinac Island in 1839. They made friends with a few Ottawa and Chippewa Indians living nearby. The following year they established a school with the help of geologist, explorer and ethnologist Henry Schoolcraft.

Rev. Dougherty moved on to Omena across the bay in 1852 to minister to a larger band of Indians, leaving behind the "Old Mission."

The history lesson doesn't stop there, however. Located on the 45th Parallel, exactly halfway between the North Pole and the Equator, the bay-warmed microclimate of the peninsula proved ideal for orchards and fruit, especially cherries, which is how Traverse City came to be known as the Cherry Capital of the World.

But a bigger revelation came in 1974 when Edward O'Keefe, Jr. of **Chateau Grand Traverse** began planting wine varietal grapes, including Pinot Noir, Chardonnay and Riesling. The peninsula was recognized as an American Viticultural Area in 1987 and has been piling on new wineries ever since. At last count there were seven.

SOUR GRAPES

Not everyone is thrilled by the sight of cyclists enjoying a ride on Old Mission Peninsula, which has seen a steady rise in development and traffic since the 1980s. A number of former orchards have been turned into upscale housing developments, and you'll see some of the area's most opulent mansions on Peninsula Drive.

The influx of residents and the boom in cycling's popularity are sometimes at loggerheads. Some residents have complained about cyclists riding three-abreast and obstructing the road (under Michigan law, cyclists can ride no more than two-abreast). There have also been complaints about testosterone-addled cyclists flipping drivers off and vice-versa. Be mindful of the situation and ride defensively.

CYCLE CAMARADERIE

If you're looking for a thrilling ride out the peninsula while rubbing elbows (literally) with some of the best cyclists in the region, you'll find it at the **Cherry Capital Cycling Club's** Monday night rides which start at 6 p.m. at the high school parking lot.

Typically, there are advanced, intermediate and easy-going groups making runs of 40, 30 and 20-25 miles. A women-only **She Bikes** group takes off from the lot around the same time. Each ride is preceded by a safety talk laying down the rules and regs about not crossing the center line and other precautions.

Count on getting dropped if you ride with the advanced 40-mile group unless you're an experienced racer in top condition. This group hammers at speeds over 20mph all the way to the lighthouse and back.

A better bet for first-timers is to ride with the intermediate 30-mile group. If you get dropped -- and many riders do -- no biggie; just pedal back on your own and savor the scenery.

The rides are intended for CCCC members only, although many non-members tag along. Be a sport and join the club.

As for amenities on the peninsula, they are few, this being farm country. But there's a general store in the burg of Old Mission, a market in Mapleton, and you can catch lunch at the **Old Mission Tavern** on Center Road, or at the **Jolly Pumpkin** winery and brewpub at Bower's Harbor.

You can also visit the wineries of the peninsula on your bike. But how would you pack a bottle of two of Pinot Gris for the way back?

Web: http://www.wineriesofoldmission.com
http://www.cherrycapitalcyclingclub.org/

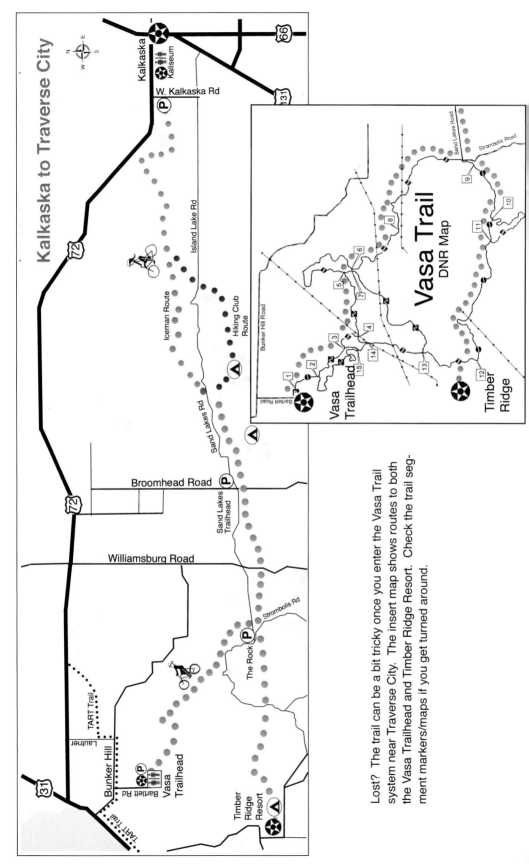

Kalkaska to Traverse City

Vasa Trail
DNR Map

Lost? The trail can be a bit tricky once you enter the Vasa Trail system near Traverse City. The insert map shows routes to both the Vasa Trailhead and Timber Ridge Resort. Check the trail segment markers/maps if you get turned around.

Kalkaska to TC

Distance: 29 miles
Bike recommendation: Mountain bike or fat bike
Essentials: tool & tire kit, chain link, compass or GPS system, phone, energy foods, 2 water bottles, first aid kit, blaze orange or fluorescent clothing in fall hunting season.
Traffic: None
Difficulty: Tough

More than 5,000 mountain bikers tear down a network of trails from Kalkaska to Traverse City in the Iceman Cometh Challenge, held each year on the first Saturday in November.

The race fills up in a matter of minutes when the website begins accepting applications at the end of February.

But if you can't get in the race you can still ride the heavily-forested route between Kalkaska and TC along the Iceman trail, which was improved by the Grand Traverse Hiking Club in 2009. The route connects the Vasa cross-country ski trail to pathways in the Sand Lakes Quiet Area, winding up on the Kalkaska Area Recreation Trail (KART).

As you'll see on the map, the Hiking Club trail diverts south from the Iceman route in order to offer camping on Guernsey Lake and the Sand Lakes Quiet Area. Either route will get ya there.

The start of the trail from Kalkaska is mostly flat with a few gentle hills. You'll see a parking lot for the trailhead off W. Kalkaska Road just west of the **Kaliseum** activity center on M-72.

Don't expect many crossroads on this route: About two-thirds of the way through, you'll come to Broomhead Road, followed by a series of hills. Then you'll cross Williamsburg Road, with the hills getting more intense. The hills continue all the way to the **Vasa Trailhead** off Bartlett Road in Acme. You can also divert to **Timber Ridge Resort**, a campground which is where the Iceman ends.

Caution! There are considerable twists and turns once you hit the area of the **Vasa Trail**, which is a confusing spaghetti tangle between the trailhead and Timber Ridge Resort. Stay alert to the trail marker maps as you near the end of your ride. Also note that Sand Lakes Road and Island Lake Road aren't much more than

Halfway point at the Iceman.

two-tracks through the forest, and sandy ones at that.

There's something to be said for starting in TC and riding to Kalkaska if you want to get those hills out of the way early on while you're still fresh. Also worth noting, the Iceman race is held in early November because that's generally when the ground frosts up enough to make this sandy trail more manageable.

What will you see along the route? Trees, trees and more trees, with the possibility of the occasional hunter, hiker or cyclists training for the Iceman. Oh yeah, you might also see some hills out there...

LOST & FOUND

Although the trail is fairly well marked, it's still easy to get lost out there. Often, there are diverging paths and it's not always easy to figure which is the correct route. Even with experienced Iceman racers for guides we managed to get turned around a time or two on a training ride, especially on the Vasa network at the end of the route.

You can't get lost for long, however, if you take a compass or a GPS system. Highway M-72 with a broad bike shoulder back to the TART Trail in Williamsburg is just a few miles to the north if you get totally turned around.

Even more important is to bring along plenty of water and some energy snacks. This route includes many winding switchbacks and can be quite slow-going, hot and humid. You may be out there a lot longer than you anticipate -- take at least two water bottles and/or a sizable camelback.

I'd also recommend taking a spare chain link kit in case your chain snaps while torquing out on the sandy conditions along the route -- a common enough experience in the Iceman.

And speaking of sand, it's also advisable to ride this route with a friend or two since there are numerous sand-traps along the way that can stop your bike dead-cold while you're flying along the trail. I've had a couple of friends suffer broken bones and near-death experiences after hitting these pits.

Be alert to the fact that bow-hunters tend to be out in force in the Sand Lakes Quiet Area during the fall. Bright colors and some chatter while riding are recommended lest you become a target of one of these camo-clad Rambos. They can be an alarming sight, and chances are they won't be pleased to see you either.

Web: www.iceman.com

Notes:

Leelanau County

Local cycle racers, triathletes and bike touring fans have been riding "The County" for decades. You'll find relatively light traffic in Leelanau County, with vistas of orchards and vineyards and plenty of opportunities for hill-training to get your quads in top shape.

There's a spaghetti-tangle of routes to enjoy; you could spend all summer exploring Leelanau, and many cyclists do just that. Whatever you do, don't attempt riding The County without tools, a tire kit and pump -- the closest bike shops are in Traverse City.

Don't Miss:

- The Leelanau Trail
- The Maple City Run
- Around Lake Leelanau
- TC to Leland
- Suttons Bay to Northport
- Sleeping Bear Heritage Trail
- Around Glen Lake

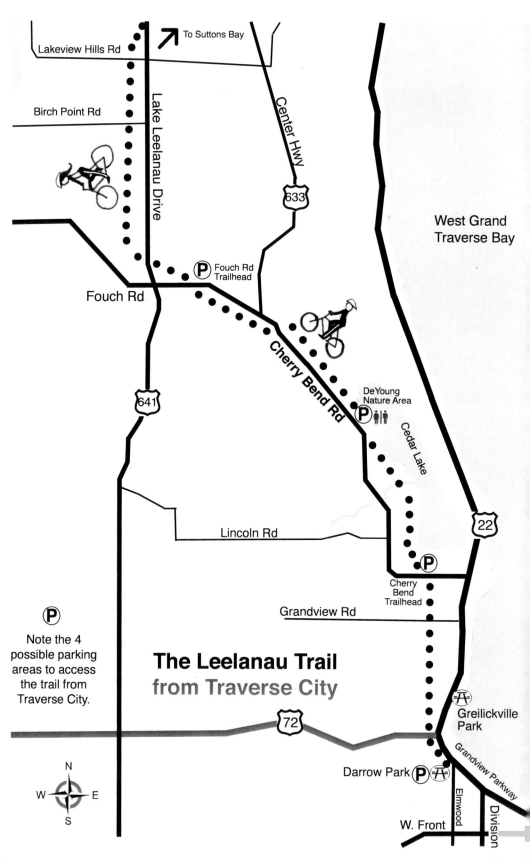

To Suttons Bay

Lakeview Hills Rd

Birch Point Rd

Lake Leelanau Drive

Center Hwy

633

West Grand
Traverse Bay

P Fouch Rd
Trailhead

Fouch Rd

Cherry Bend Rd

641

DeYoung
Nature Area

P

Cedar Lake

22

Lincoln Rd

P

Cherry
Bend
Trailhead

P

Grandview Rd

The Leelanau Trail
from Traverse City

Note the 4
possible parking
areas to access
the trail from
Traverse City.

72

Greilickville
Park

Darrow Park P

Grandview Parkway

Elmwood

Division

W. Front

N
W   E
S

The Leelanau Trail

Distance: 17 miles
Bike recommendation: All good
Essentials: Tool & tire kit, money for lunch
Traffic: None
Difficulty: Easy. Round-trip can be a challenge for newbies

Ask any cyclist what's the best ride out of Traverse City and most will likely agree on the Leelanau Trail.

Hundreds of cyclists ride the trail each day, starting at either end of a 17-mile route that stretches from the foot of West Grand Traverse Bay to the Village of Suttons Bay.

Many cyclists park at Darrow Park on the west side of TC and take the trail north past Tom's supermarket. Another popular parking spot is the trailhead on Cherry Bend Road, 3 miles down the trail. You can also continue down Cherry Bend to another trailhead parking lot where the road turns into Fouch Road.

The trail runs through marshy woodlands past Cedar Lake and then begins a gentle climb through the rolling hills, farms and vineyards of Leelanau County. Don't be surprised if you find the wind in your face the whole way out and back -- the ever-shifting wind seems to be one of the quirks of what the locals call "the County."

The 10-foot-wide trail is paved with asphalt the entire way and there are no hazards to speak of, although on occasion you may encounter packs of overzealous locals riding at speeds of 20 mph or more. Fortunately, the speedsters tend to do their riding early in the morning and you'll hear them coming with calls of "On your left!"

On the plus side, you'll find fewer small children weaving back and forth in your path, which tends to be the case with the clusters of family groups on the TART Trail in town.

THE NIMBY BATTLE

Today, you'll find some area residents seeking new homes along the trail, both for commuting and for recreation. But when the conversion of an abandoned railway line for a linear state park

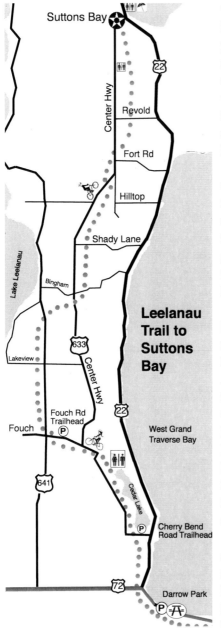

Leelanau Trail to Suttons Bay

was first proposed in the early '90s it sparked a huge not-in-my-back-yard outcry from homeowners and farmers along the route. Some made claims that rapists and burglars would use the trail to creep up on their homes; others felt the sanctity of 'their' snowmobile route would be compromised.

Trail opponents obtained resolutions condemning the trail from the village councils of Suttons Bay and Northport, as well as from four townships along the route. Michigan's DNR withdrew its support in the wake of fierce opposition and it looked like the trail was a goner.

But area cyclists refused to throw in the towel. In 1994, the abandoned rail bed was purchased for $475,000 by the non-profit Leelanau Trails Association, a volunteer organization aligned with TART in Traverse City (which owns the trail today). Even then the legal battle with the NIMBYs carried on. Rural Bingham Township spent more than $20,000 in legal fees over a zoning issue that went all the way to the state Supreme Court.

Confrontations between locals and riders arose after an unpaved mountain bike trail was established between TC and Suttons Bay. This included verbal abuse and even a booby trap that sent one rider tumbling after a ditch was dug across the trail. Today, you can still see a sign at an intersection a couple miles south of Suttons Bay that instructs riders to call the Leelanau County Sheriff if they encounter any problems.

Trail supporters prevailed in the end and the route was gradually paved in sections. Unfortunately, the rail bed running north from Suttons Bay to Northport was purchased in 1994 by the Grand Traverse Band of Ottawa and Chippewa Indians, catering to public pressure. The tribe sold it to adjacent property owners who chopped up the route with deed restrictions, preventing it from ever becoming a bike path. (The tribe has since become a strong supporter of the Sleeping Bear Heritage Trail.)

All is not lost, however; in the summer of 2014 a new stretch of trail was added a short way north of Suttons Bay to Dumas Road. Perhaps it augers better things to come.

ALL GOOD NOW

Today, the Village of Suttons Bay joyfully embraces the trail and the influx of well-heeled cyclists and the dollars they bring. There's a parking lot at the trailhead south of town just for cyclists.

You'll find a number of good restaurant/taverns in town. Check out **Boone's Prime Time** if you crave a good burger. Down the street is the **Village Inn**, offering a full menu at the oldest tavern in town. In the spring and fall you may find riders out of TC doing a **Bloody Mary Run** to the Inn for their Sunday brunch.

There's also a **Muffin Run** of cyclists every Friday at 9 a.m. in the spring through fall, riding from Grandview Road in TC to the **Blue Lotus** bakery/coffeeshop at the trailhead in Suttons Bay. Catch riders passing by the Fouch Road trailhead around 9:10 am.

No trip to Leelanau County would be complete without sampling some of its excellent wines, with Pinot Grigio being the best local grape. **Black Star Farms** is just a short hop down Revold Road a couple of miles south of Suttons Bay. They offer a fine selection of locally-made cheeses in addition to brandies and wines.

There are two options for returning to TC; either set your wheels in a southerly direction and ride, or take advantage of the bike & bus service offered by the Bay Area Transportation Authority. BATA offers a mini-bus route with bike racks for this route. Check the website below for available times of service.

Web: http://traversetrails.org/trail/leelanau-trail
http://www.bata.net

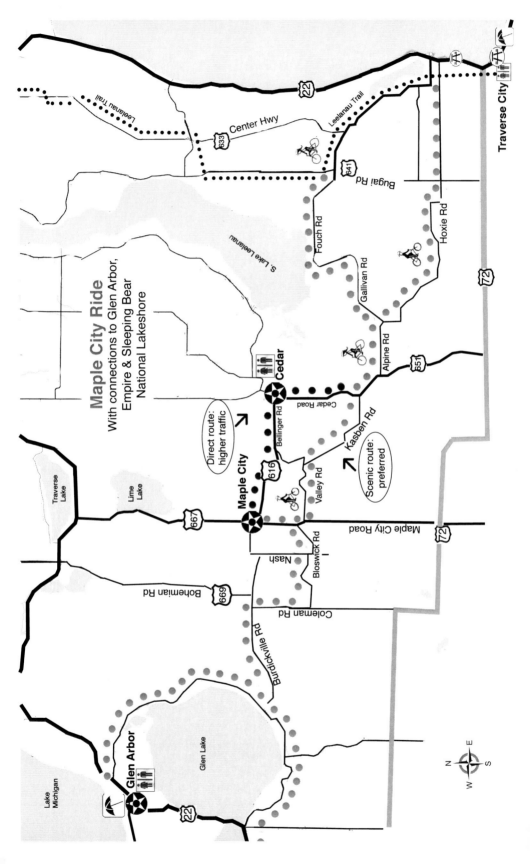

Maple City Ride
With connections to Glen Arbor, Empire & Sleeping Bear National Lakeshore

Direct route: higher traffic

Scenic route: preferred

Traverse City

Leelanau Trail

Center Hwy

533

22

Leelanau Trail

641

Bugai Rd

Fouch Rd

S. Lake Leelanau

Gallivan Rd

Hoxie Rd

72

Alpine Rd

Cedar

551

Cedar Road

Kasben Rd

Bellinger Rd

616

Maple City

Valley Rd

667

Lime Lake

Traverse Lake

Nash

Bloswick Rd

Maple City Road

72

Coleman Rd

Bohemian Rd

669

Burdickville Rd

Glen Arbor

Glen Lake

22

Lake Michigan

N
W   E
S

The Maple City Ride

Including • TC to Glen Arbor
& Sleeping Bear National Lakeshore

Distance: 35-70 mile circuit
Bike Preference: Road bike
Essentials: tool & tire kit, sunscreen, fluorescent jersey, water, energy foods, phone
Traffic: Light to medium
Difficulty: Semi-tough due to distance, hills

The Maple City ride has been a popular cycling route out of Traverse City for decades, even though many cyclists never actually visit the town. Basically, this route gives you an introduction to what the county has to offer and serves as the gateway to riding further on to Glen Arbor, Empire or the Sleeping Bear National Lakeshore.

It's 17 miles to Maple City, give or take a few depending on your route.

There are a couple of ways to bike to and from Traverse City. I prefer to ride the slightly longer route out and return on the shorter route. Take your pick.

Heading north on the Leelanau Trail from TC, you'll come to the second parking lot on Cherry Bend Road, which turns into Fouch Road (614). Take a left and head west on Fouch. Or, you can ride another half-mile down the trail and double back south to Fouch at the next intersection.

Fouch Road curves around to become S. Weisler and E. Gallivan roads. Back in the '80s, this stretch served as a 10-mile out-and-back time-trial course for local triathletes who hammered up the long hill you'll find here.

Turn right at E. Alpine and you'll come to the tiny Solon Cemetery at the intersection of 616. Remember this spot, as you may be returning this way.

Now you have options: either a direct route to Cedar and Maple City along some busy roads, or a more scenic route which bypasses both towns.

TO CEDAR

If you wish to visit Cedar, head north on 651. This stretch has the most traffic you'll find on the route, but fortunately, there's a shoulder on the road that accommodates bikes.

If it's open, be sure to stop at the **Cedar Sol Hydro Farm Taco Stand** on the hill just before Cedar for a home-style Mexican meal or snack. Otherwise, carry on downhill to the village. Here, you'll find a soft-serve ice-cream hut. The **Cedar City Market** is also a good bet for snacks, and next door you'll find **Pleva's Meats**, home of the locally-famous cherry sausage and burger.

Cedar got its name back in the lumber era when it was parked in the middle of a cedar forest. Today, it's best known for the Pleva's brand, and for the **Cedar Polka Festival** held in early July -- a white folks' bacchanalia of polka dancing under a big top, powered by beer and sausage.

From Cedar, you take a left at the intersection at Bellinger Road (616) and head west a little more than 3 miles to Maple City.

Here, you'll find **Peg Town Station**, noted for its hearty breakfasts, lunch and pizza. The café honors Maple City's original name, Peg Town, where a long-gone factory made wooden pegs used in the construction of shoes back in the 1800s. Another stop for thirsty cyclists is **Kerby's Bar & Grill.**

Otherwise, you're basically in the middle of nowhere with not much to see or do. But from Maple City you can head west down Burdickville Road to connect to Big Glen Lake and the routes to Glen Arbor, Sleeping Bear National Lakeshore and Empire.

BETTER OPTION

If you don't care to visit Cedar, a quieter and more scenic route is the one used by the Leelanau Harvest Tour and the Cherry Capital Cycling Club.

Here, you head west down Kasben Road off 651. Follow the quiet roads shown on the map to Maple City and beyond.

If you're returning to TC, cycle back to the Solon Cemetery and head east on Alpine past the intersection at E. Gallivan. You'll connect to E. Hoxie Road and a long uphill climb through cornfields to the heights above TC. You'll be happy to see the downhill run when the road diverts down E. Grandview. The road crosses the Leelanau Trail in Greilickville just before it hits M-22.

TOUR OPTION:
For a longer version of this route and the camaraderie of hundreds of cyclists, consider the **Leelanau Harvest Tour**, which takes place on the third Sunday in September. Hosted by the Cherry Capital Cycling Club, the tour offers 20, 40, 65 and 100-mile options. For details, see **www.cherrycapitalcyclingclub.org**

Around South Lake Leelanau

Distance: About 50 miles
Bike recommendation: Road bike
Essentials: tool & tire kit, sunscreen, fluorescent jersey, water, energy foods, phone
Traffic: Light to medium
Difficulty: Semi-tough due to distance, hills

This is my favorite Leelanau ride, making a circuit of 50 or so miles along some of the county's quietest roads and some of its finest scenery.

Lake Leelanau is actually two lakes: North and South, a 22-mile waterway connected by a channel at the Village of Lake Leelanau. For our purposes, we'll be riding around the larger South Lake Leelanau, which is about 12 miles long.

Start on the Leelanau Trail in TC and head north to E. Lakeview Hills Road. Take a left; the road will wind around north, connecting to S. Lake Leelanau Drive (641). This will take you all the way to the Village of Lake Leelanau.

Unfortunately, you won't be able to see the lake on the east side, unless you stop at **Fountain Point,** a grand, historic resort established in 1889. Today, it also serves as a concert venue and rowing camp.

Fountain Point is located near the north end of S. Lake Leelanau. You can also catch views of the lake a short ways north at a boat launch, which has outhouses for those in need of relief.

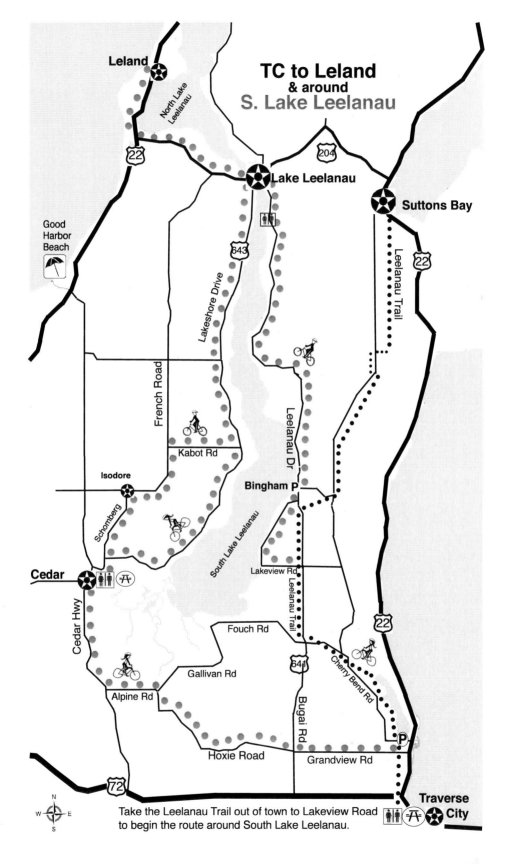

TC to Leland
& around
S. Lake Leelanau

Leland

North Lake Leelanau

22

Good Harbor Beach

204

Lake Leelanau

Suttons Bay

22

643

Leelanau Trail

Lakeshore Drive

French Road

Leelanau Dr

Kabot Rd

Isodore

Bingham P

Schomberg

Lakeview Rd

South Lake Leelanau

Cedar

Leelanau Trail

Cedar Hwy

Fouch Rd

22

Gallivan Rd

64

Cherry Bend Rd

Alpine Rd

Bugai Rd

Hoxie Road

Grandview Rd

72

N
W   E
S

Take the Leelanau Trail out of town to Lakeview Road to begin the route around South Lake Leelanau.

Traverse City

Arriving at the Village of Lake Leelanau, you'll find **Dick's Pour House**, an atmospheric bar offering great burgers. Writer Jim Harrison used to hold forth here when he resided in the village back in the '80s.

The return trip takes you through town to 643 South. You'll catch views of the lake as you ride the hills above the shore, with a good stop being at the **Bel Lago** winery near the southern end. This link takes you to 645, just outside Cedar. To return to TC, take the Alpine Road route suggested in the Maple City Ride.

ALTERNATIVE ROUTE

Some cyclists like to turn right on Kabot Road just before Bel Lago Winery on highway 643. This takes you to French Road and the picturesque Holy Rosary Church.

This church at the crossroads of Isadore was the site of the 1907 disappearance of Sister Mary Janina. Her bones were found under a pile of lumber in the church basement in 1918. It turns out the priest's housekeeper killed the nun -- jealous that she was spending too much time with Father Andrew Bieniawski. The housekeeper was convicted in 1919.

From the church, ride south to Cedar and follow the above instructions home.

Traverse City to Leland

Distance: 35 miles one-way
Bike Preference: Road bike
Essentials: tool & tire kit, sunscreen, fluorescent jersey, water, energy foods, phone
Traffic: Medium
Difficulty: Semi-tough due to distance

Following the same route you took to the Village of Lake Leelanau, head west on 204 until it intersects with M-22. It's a busy road, but fortunately, there's a wide bike lane.

Turn right on M-22, being careful of traffic, and proceed a couple

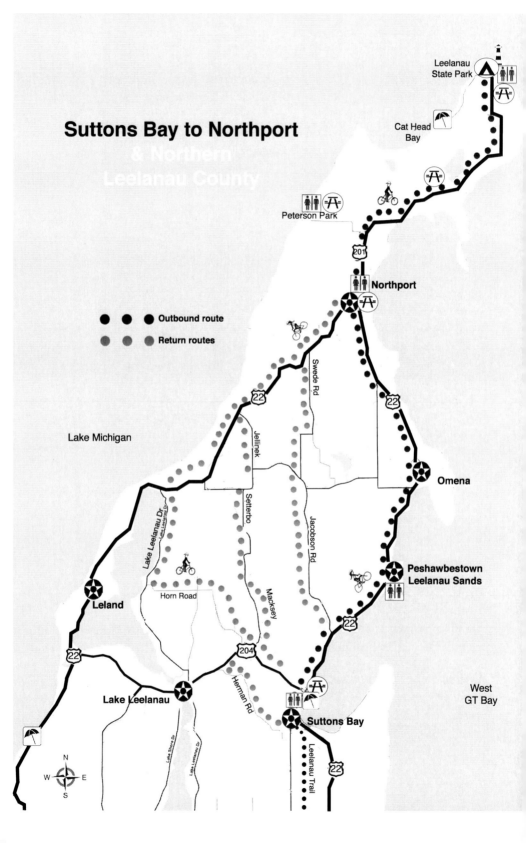

of miles into Leland.

Home to the **Fishtown** boardwalk and many shops and restaurants, Leland is a tourist's wonderland. Enjoy breakfast at **The Early Bird**, or the fancier and more atmospheric **Riverside Inn**. Lunch on the deck by the dam at **The Cove** can be memorable if you're there in the fall when the salmon are jumping. Or, check out **The Bluebird**, a favorite with locals which has a good selection of local fish.

If you're feeling adventurous and up for a longer ride, consider heading south down M-22 a few miles to **Good Harbor Beach** just past Good Harbor Vineyards tasting room & market. This is one of the most popular beaches in Northern Michigan with miles of sandy shores curving out of sight in both directions.

Suttons Bay to Northport

Distance: 24 to 50+ mile options
Bike Recommendation: Road bike or hybrid
Essentials: tool & tire kit, sunscreen, fluorescent jersey, water, energy foods, phone
Traffic: Light to medium
Difficulty: Easy to semi-tough, depending on distance

Chances are you won't find many other cyclists riding to the tip of Leelanau County, nor many cars, and that's one of the joys of riding through the northern center of the peninsula past miles of rolling farmland and orchards.

The caveat is the stretch of several miles along M-22 from Suttons Bay to at least the **Leelanau Sands Casino** in Peshawbestown where you're likely to encounter traffic on a narrow, unsafe road. It's advisable to ride this stretch on an early Sunday morning or a quiet weekday, or simply avoid it and take one of the 'back ways' to Northport shown on the map.

It's a straightforward route, riding north out of Suttons Bay on the new trail to Dumas Road. Head 12 miles on M-22, past Peshawbestown and Omena. Beyond Northport, keep riding north on 201 if you wish to pedal to the tip o' the Leelanau.

Along with Omena, Peshawbestown was the site of an Indian village long before white settlers showed up. The village was an impoverished rural ghetto of shacks and dilapidated mobile homes into the early 1980s. Then, the Grand Traverse Band of Ottawa and Chippewa Indians won the right to establish a bingo parlor on their 12.5-acre reservation. That gaming enterprise was a huge hit, leading to the first Indian casino in Michigan. Today, the larger **Turtle Creek Casino** in Williamsburg, west of TC, has stolen some of the Sands' thunder, but its showroom still hosts occasional concerts by nationally-touring acts and its gaming tables remain a draw for Leelanau residents and tourists.

Carrying on, you'll pass Omena which sports a harborside bar and the **Tamarack Gallery** -- one of the best in Northern Michigan. A few miles on you'll roll into Northport and the sole reason many cyclists ride here: **Barb's Bakery.** Lodged in a 130-year-old building and open 7 days a week, Barb's offers cinnamon twist rolls to die for.

After falling into decline in the '90s and '00s, Northport has been on the rebound in recent years with many new businesses and restaurants worth exploring.

You can ride on another 5 miles to the tip of the peninsula. Along the way you'll find a hiking trail circling Mud Lake which winds through the forest to beautiful **Cat Head Bay** on a secluded stretch of Lake Michigan. Further on is Leelanau State Park and a lighthouse at the tip of the peninsula.

CHOICES, CHOICES

Heading back south you can explore the tip of Leelanau County via numerous options. Veer right on M-22 at Northport and ride toward Leland. A great stop on M-22 is **Fischer's Happy Hour** for burgers & brews. You can ride down the east shore of North Lake Leelanau to 204 and back to Suttons Bay on the highway. Or, head down the center of the peninsula through remote farms and orchards.

If you wish to avoid busy 204, consider taking Herman Road the back way into Suttons Bay (see map); but be forewarned, this route packs a killer hill that will test your weary legs. Have fun -- most of these interior roads are 'all yours.'

Sleeping Bear Heritage Trail

Distance: 4 miles to Glen Arbor, 5.5 miles to Empire
Bike recommendation: All good
Essentials: Sunscreen, money for coffee or ice cream
Traffic: None
Difficulty: Easy as pie

It's unlikely that any bike path in Northern Michigan packs more smiles per mile than the Sleeping Bear Heritage Trail. On any sunny day in the summer you'll find tourists from all over the world grinning from ear-to-ear with the exhilaration of riding this new trail through "the most beautiful place in America."

That last bit was courtesy of ABC's "Good Morning America" show, with more than 100,000 viewers voting the Sleeping Bear National Lakeshore the top spot for scenery in 2011. Interest in the park surged after the announcement, with more than 1.7 million visitors putting it on their bucket list in 2012. Those numbers are only expected to grow.

THE BACKSTORY

The 35-mile long park was created in 1973 through the support of former U.S. Senator Phil Hart. Initially, there was a great deal of local opposition to the park, since it required the appropriation of private property; some businesses, such as dune buggy operators, were shut down. But a number of cottage owners and enterprises such as The Homestead ski resort were grandfathered in and remain to this day.

Today, the park encompasses 111 square miles, 64 miles of beaches, 100 miles of hiking trails, 26 inland lakes, two islands, a river, and the villages of Empire and Glen Arbor. It also boasts the tallest dunes in America.

There are plans underway to create a new **Bay-to-Bay Trail** through the backcountry which will allow backpackers to hike 30 miles through the park. But more exciting for cyclists is the ongoing effort to create a 27-mile cycle path that will run from south of

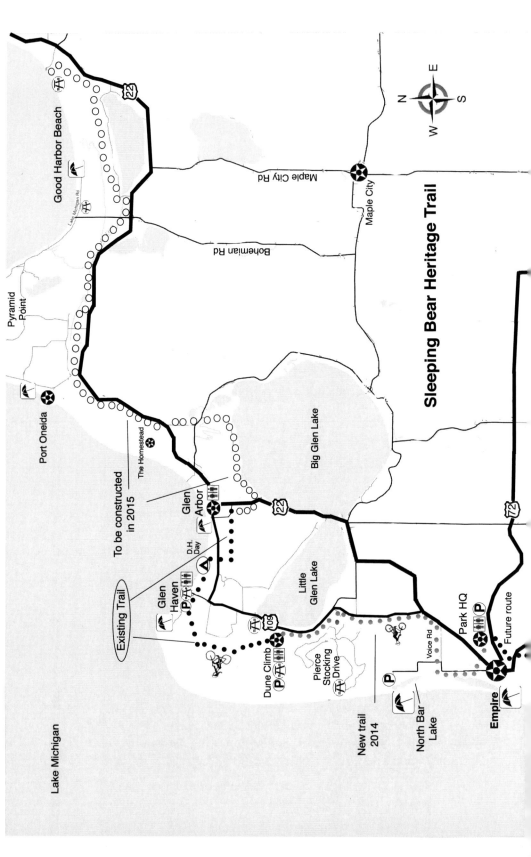

Sleeping Bear Heritage Trail

Empire all the way to the beach at Good Harbor Bay.

Eventually, it's projected that the Sleeping Bear Heritage Trail will attract 350,000 cyclists each year, but fortunately, not all at once.

GLEN HAVEN

The first leg of the trail was completed in 2012 and runs 4 miles north to Glen Arbor from the Dune Climb where you'll also find a bathroom and changing facility. The trail rolls through a series of forested sandhills before reaching your first stop, the historic museum village of Glen Haven.

Established in 1857, Glen Haven boomed after the Civil War with local industries including lumbering, fishing and ice harvesting on Glen Lake. A huge dock (now long gone) was constructed to serve passing steamers. Residents also benefited by purloining timber and other cargo that rolled off the deck of ships in storms.

Today, you'll find a **maritime museum** of the old U.S. Lifesaving Service which operated from this point. The swift currents of the Manitou Passage were notorious shipwreck hazards and the Coast Guard crews at Glen Haven and on South Manitou Island had their work cut out, rescuing survivors in longboats rowed from the shore. A Lyle cannon was also used to fire a rescue line 1,200 feet to ships going down.

You'll enjoy good views of the Manitou islands here, so named because the Ottawa and Chippewa Indians believed they were alive with magical spirits. Catch the boat out of Leland for a day trip or a campout and you're sure to agree.

These islands are the bear cubs of Indian legend. Once, long ago, a mama bear and her two cubs fled a huge forest fire in Wisconsin, swimming across Lake Michigan. Exhausted, the mother climbed a hill on the eastern shore of the big lake, only to die of heartbreak when her cubs drowned within sight of land. Impressed by her courage, the Great Spirit created the Manitou islands in memory of the cubs and raised a huge mound of sand to honor the mother bear.

Glen Haven is also the closest crossing point to South Manitou Island for sea kayakers and canoeists, but don't try this alone or without an expert level of deep water rescue for if and when your boat flips. Even on a clear day these waters can churn to ragged,

8-to-10-foot waves in a matter of minutes owing to Michigan's fickle weather. In 2013 an 8-year-old boy lost his life after his father ignored advice not to attempt the crossing and their canoe flipped a mile from shore.

Beyond Glen Haven the trail runs through the D.H. Day Campground, named after an early pioneer. Carry on across highway 109 to the artsy tourist town of Glen Arbor, the amenities of which are detailed in the section "Around Glen Lake," page 53.

SOUTH TO EMPIRE

An new 5.5-mile trail from the Dune Climb to Empire was set for completion in July, 2014 as this book went to press. This leg of the trail passes the beach at North Bar Lake, one of the most popular swimming holes in Northern Michigan. When it's too windy or cold to swim in Lake Michigan, beachgoers can always count on a pleasant experience at North Bar Lake, which is sheltered by a canopy of dunes. There's a short stream from North Bar to Lake Michigan which is especially thrilling (and safe) for kids.

The new trail also passes scenic Pierce Stocking Drive; if you're up for a few strenuous hill climbs you can cycle all the way to the lookout at the top of the dunes for vistas of Lake Michigan.

Continuing on to the park headquarters in Empire you'll find interactive displays of what the park has to offer, including its wildlife and natural history. In town, **Friendly's Tavern** makes a good lunch stop, as does the Empire **Village Inn** on M-22 which is favored by locals for its pizza. **Sleeping Bear Surf & Kayak** also makes for a cool stopover.

LOOKING AHEAD

Also scheduled for completion in late 2014 is a new 5-mile stretch of trail from Glen Arbor north to the historic farming community of Port Oneida. From there, an additional 3 miles of trail will be constructed in 2015 to the gorgeous, but little-known Good Harbor Beach at Bohemian Road, north of Maple City.

For a cyclist, it's almost dizzying to think that by 2015 you'll be able to ride through this lovely park all the way from Empire more than 17 miles north to Good Harbor Beach, with the eventual trail to span 27 miles. A final stretch will pass Little Traverse Lake to another popular beach on Good Harbor, south of Leland.

But the freedom to ride through Sleeping Bear National Lakeshore doesn't come for free. $775,000 in private donations must be raised to match $4.25 million in public funds to make the Sleeping Bear Heritage Trail a reality. If you'd like to make a donation, you can find opportunities online through the **Friends of Sleeping Bear Dunes,** or at the new Donation Plaza at the Dune Climb. And, of course, be sure to buy a day pass or annual pass to support the park.

Web: http://sleepingbeartrail.org
http://www.nps.gov/slbe/index.htm

Around Glen Lake

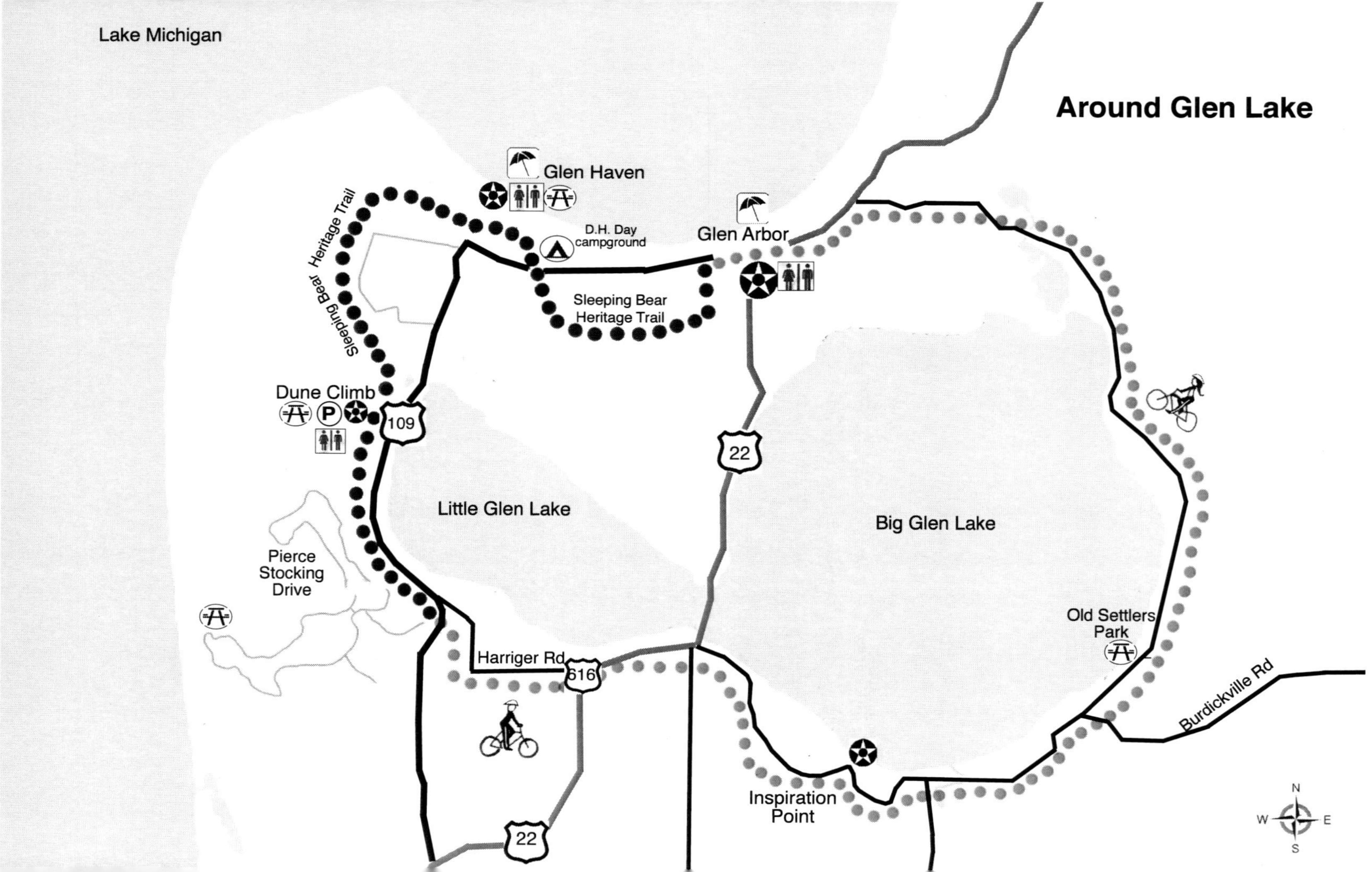

Lake Michigan

Glen Haven

Glen Arbor

D.H. Day campground

Sleeping Bear Heritage Trail

Sleeping Bear Heritage Trail

Dune Climb

Pierce Stocking Drive

Little Glen Lake

Big Glen Lake

Inspiration Point

Old Settlers Park

Harriger Rd

Burdickville Rd

22

616

109

22

Around Glen Lake

Distance: 17 miles
Bike recommendation: Road bike or hybrid
Essentials: Check your brakes, lunch money, tube & tire kit
Traffic: Light to medium (passing through Glen Arbor)
Difficulty: Fairly easy, with one big hill

This is one of Northern Michigan's most blissful roadbike rides, making the circuit and Big and Little Glen Lake, with fabulous views to be had at the top of a whopper hill called Inspiration Point.

You can ride a hybrid or mountain bike, but I prefer to give my roadbike a spin on this route because traffic tends to be light and you can really get flying on a few downhill stretches.

Glen Lake, like Torch Lake to the northeast, claims the sobriquet of being one of the top-10 "most beautiful" lakes in the world, also citing *National Geographic* as a source. Take a dip in its crystal-blue sandy-bottom waters and you'll be tempted to agree -- it's a clear as snorkeling the Caribbean.

You can leave from Glen Arbor, where parking is free, but I prefer to start and end at the mammoth Dune Climb in the Sleeping Bear National Lakeshore.

Be sure to climb the 400-foot-high dune (on foot, that is); it's not as bad as it looks, especially for a tough biker like yourself. At the annual **M-22 Challenge** triathlon held here in early June, participants run up this dune (struggle might be the better word) before riding around the Glen lakes and finishing with a canoe or kayak paddle. Be sure to check out the **M-22** store in Glen Arbor for cool clothes and paraphernalia relating to the recreation lifestyle.

MAKING THE LOOP

Since this is a circuit, you can do this ride in either direction, but the counterclockwise route is the better of the two because it offers a gentler climb up Inspiration Point and also wraps up near Glen Arbor for a lunch or snack.

Head south on highway 109. At Harriger Road (616) you'll take a left (careful of those potholes!) and proceed left on Welch Road to M-22. Keep going past the bridge at the isthmus between Little and Big Glen lakes (good for a stop) and head along W. Macfarlane Road (still 616).

Now you've got a nice, long climb through a shady forest to the top of Inspiration Point. The Point is just over 900 feet above sea level. You're not actually climbing that high, since the Glen lakes are already several hundred feet above sea level, but reaching the top feels like an accomplishment.

Whatever you do, be sure to stop at the little turnoff at the top of the hill for spectacular views of the lakes, the Manitou islands and Alligator Hill, which was created by the retreat of glaciers in the last ice age. On a clear day you can even see the Fox islands, far out in the Lake Michigan Archipelago.

ON TO GLEN ARBOR

It's a straightforward ride from here on. If you're a real speed demon you should have no problem hitting 40mph or so going down the steep side of the hill. Meeker souls will want to take it easy on this stretch. In any case, make sure your brakes are in good working order before you take the plunge.

Dude, where's my bike? The M-22 Challenge includes a run to the top of the Sleeping Bear Dunes before cycling 17 miles around Glen Lake.

The road soon turns into highway 675 and carries on around Big Glen Lake. As is the case with the Torch Lake ride, you'll rarely catch a peep of the lake through the high-priced homes which line its shores. Your best bet for a view is stopping at the **Old Settlers Park**, a rustic picnic grounds on the southeastern shore.

The route carries on past the dam on the Crystal River where many kayakers and canoeists put in for a float into town. This paddle is very shallow, but also very scenic, and well-worth your time if you care to rent a kayak after your ride at one of the riverside outfits in Glen Arbor.

In Glen Arbor you'll have to negotiate a maze of SUV-driving tourists, most of whom seem to come from Chicago or the wealthier suburbs of Detroit. Exercise caution here as tourists in general throughout northwestern lower Michigan tend to be looking at everything but where they're driving.

There are several good lunch options in Glen Arbor: **Art's Bar** is noted for its burgers (but beware, they don't except credit cards); meanwhile, veggie and health-oriented options are available at the **Good Harbor Grill**. The deck at the **Boone Docks** also makes for a lively scene, especially during the late afternoon and early evening when live acoustic music is performed by local pickers. Great coffee stops are offered at **Cherry Republic** or the **Leelanau County Roasting Company**.

WRAPPING IT UP

You can ride the road back, but a better option is taking the new 4-mile Sleeping Bear Heritage Trail, completed through the woodlands of the park in 2012. It's a gorgeous trail, wandering through a forest of mixed hardwoods, **D.H. Day State Park** campground, Glen Haven Historic Village and a series of rolling sand hills back to the Dune Climb parking lot. (See details about Glen Haven in the section on the Sleeping Bear Heritage Trail.)

To catch the trail, head a short way south down M-22 from Glen Arbor and look for it on the right. Alternatively, you can catch it off Forest Haven Drive, just a block west of town.

Feeling good after your ride? How 'bout another hike up to the top of the Dune Climb? Well, maybe next time...

Web: http://sleepingbeartrail.org

Notes:

Benzie County

Benzie County is the smallest county in Michigan, but holds some of its biggest secrets. It's a rural paradise blessed with some of the state's most beautiful beaches, artful beach towns, scenic rivers, outdoor adventures and dining options.

Add to that list some spectacular cycling routes on quiet roads or through dense forests. Blissful Benzie will keep you busy on many cycling day trips, but shhhh... let's keep this our little secret.

Don't Miss:

- The Betsie Valley Trail
- Beulah to Thompsonville
- Biking M-22 to Glen Arbor
- TC to the Benzie Coast
- Around Crystal Lake
- Interlochen to
  Frankfort Loop

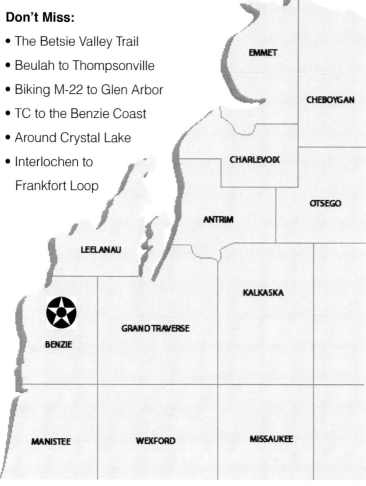

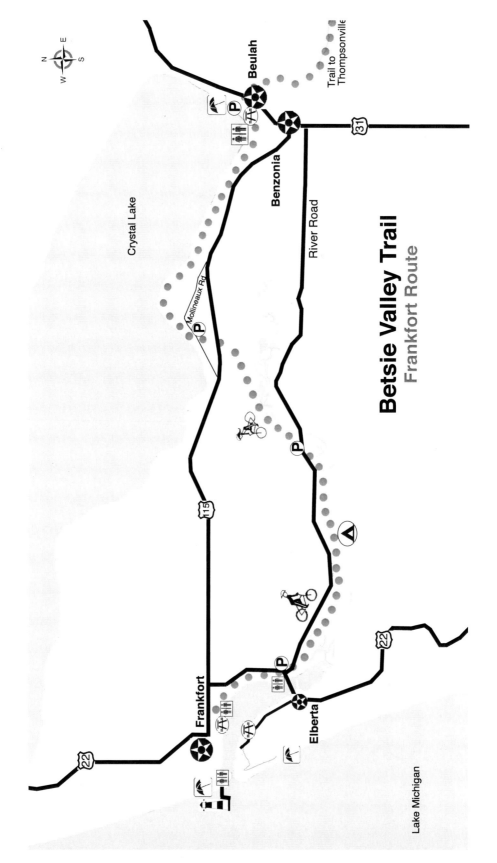

Betsie Valley Trail
Frankfort Route

The Betsie Valley Trail

Distance: 8-9 miles -- Beulah to Frankfort route
Bike recommendation: Hybrid, mountain bike or cruiser
Essentials: Money for ice cream or coffee
Traffic: None
Difficulty: Easy

The Betsie Valley Trail in Benzie County has it all: gorgeous scenery and a beach town destination with dining options priced for every budget. It's a 'must' family adventure or romantic ride for two.

Most cyclists start at the beach-side park in the village of Beulah on Crystal Lake. Grab a slice of home-style pizza at the **East Shore Market** or a cuppa' coffee at **Blue Caribou** to savor the local flavor and you're set to ride.

The trail along the former Ann Arbor Railroad Corridor heads west from the park on the west side of town. The trail also heads east past the railroad depot for those wishing to ride to Thompsonville. The total trail is 22 miles long.

THE BACKSTORY

Like the Leelanau Trail, the Betsie Valley Trail is much beloved today, but had its roots in controversy.

The trail was first proposed in the early '90s as a rails-to-trails partnership between Benzie County and Michigan's DNR. A group of trail advocates known as the Friends of the Betsie Valley Trail was organized in 1993, with volunteers lending a hand to keep the project moving. The first section of the trail was paved in 2000.

But some of the wealthy residents of Crystal Lake were displeased with the idea of a trail running past "their" lakeshore. Thus, a 10-year legal battle that was resolved with an agreement to pave the beginning of the trail with limestone for 2.5 miles west of Beulah past the private homes along the water.

The limestone segment makes it difficult to ride this section of the trail on a skinny-tire bike, especially since there are sand traps here and there. It can be done if you take your time and use a little care, but you'll want to unclip your shoes.

Ironically, even many hybrid and mountain bike cyclists opt to ride on the road alongside the limestone path, which also tends to irk the locals. Don't be surprised if someone gives you a toot or some 'attitude' and exercise caution when the road turns into a single lane.

Once you're free of the town you'll find glorious scenes of Crystal Lake and a remote beach which beckons for a quick dip.

The asphalt pavement starts at Mollineaux Road where you cross a small creek. A short distance on is busy Frankfort Highway 115. Take care to watch your kids at this intersection, since vehicles are generally traveling 60 mph or more.

The trail climbs gently through a lush forest and then wends its way along the Betsie River with several turnoffs where you can spot paddlers going by.

SOME SIGHTS

Speaking of which, if kayaking or canoeing is in your plans, this run of the Betsie River is exceptional for the wildlife and birds along its heavily-forested banks. There's a put-in a couple of miles to the east at a small bridge on River Road and a take-out at the bigger bridge where you cross on your bike.

Once you cross River Road it's a flat ride all the way to Elberta with scenery that includes the marshlands of the Betsie River just before it reaches Betsie Bay and Frankfort harbor (also known as Betsie Lake).

There are also a few worthwhile attractions on River Road worth exploring: **Gwen Frostic's** print studio is here in a rambling, hobbit-style complex that offers the deceased artist's range of greeting cards and stationery. There's also an **alpaca farm** east of the River Road crossing which is open to visitors, and a couple miles to the east you'll find **BeeDazzled,** which offers honey, beeswax candles and a pleasant garden.

ELBERTA & FRANKFORT

Once you reach Elberta, you have a range of options. To the left along Betsie Bay is the rambling **Cabbage Shed.** Constructed in 1867, the Shed was used as a cabbage warehouse in the 1930s. It has long since been converted into one of Benzie County's most happenin' hangouts, with live music, patio dining, and one of the best burgers you'll find in Northern Michigan.

Further up the hill is the **Trick Dog** coffeehouse, offering a view of the harbor and Frankfort along with the whimsical folk art of painter and sculptor Greg Jaris.

If Frankfort is your destination, head north (right) at the River Road intersection for a 1-mile pedal into town.

The dining options in Frankfort are superb. Don't miss **The Fusion** for wallet-friendly Asian cuisine. For a taste of Frankfort's maritime heritage, you'll find memorabilia at **Dinghy's** along with an excellent BBQ pork sandwich or ribs.

Another 'must' is walking the **Frankfort's Pier**, offering a quarter-mile of strolling past fishermen to the lighthouse. The pier dates back to 1873, with the 'new' 67-foot lighthouse constructed in 1912. But don't even dream of hiking the pier if waves are breaking over its walls; in 2000 a 15-year-old boy was swept from the pier to his death. You'll see memorials to him and warnings on the life rings.

No bike ride to Frankfort is complete without a visit to the **Dairy Maid**, a soft-serve ice cream place on Frankfort Highway next to Glen's supermarket a block north of Main Street. There are fancier places in town, but you can't beat the prices here and daily specials such as lemon custard.

Web: http://www.betsievalleytrail.org

Beulah to Thompsonville

Distance: 13 miles
Bike recommendation: Hybrid or mountain bike
Essentials: tool & tire repair kit, bug spray
Traffic: None
Difficulty: Easy. Semi-tough for those unused to longer rides

This lonely stretch of trail is the sister to the far more popular Benzie-Elberta route, but it's well worth doing if you're up for the

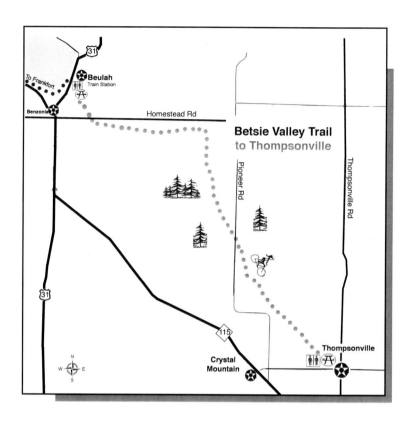

wild side of Benzie County.

The trail south of Beulah plunges into a dense forest -- in fact, some of the locals call it the Benzie Jungle -- providing opportunities for wildlife viewing. But otherwise, there's not much to see on this limestone path which runs 13 miles to Thompsonville.

Thompsonville would most likely be a ghost town today if it weren't for its colossal neighbor to the west, the **Crystal Mountain** ski resort. Even so, the town is barely there.

But in its lumber era heyday, Thompsonville was the largest city in northwestern lower Michigan, eclipsing Traverse City in size as the lumberjacks clearcut the surrounding forests. Plenty of timber went to rebuild Chicago and the cities of southern Michigan when Mrs. O'Leary's cow "tipped the lantern in the shed" in 1871. The Great Chicago Fire leveled not only the windy city, but sparks drifted across the lake to bedevil many other communities.

When the timber disappeared the town fathers of Thompsonville seized upon the idea of farming the area as a way to keep the place alive. But although the land was cleared of pine, the sandy soil proved too thin to support much in the way of agriculture. And thus, RIP Thompsonville's hopes for becoming a city of any size.

But thirsty cyclists can still grab a beer and a burger at the **Laughing Horse Saloon** just east of town and reflect on what might have been.

M-22: Frankfort to Glen Arbor

Distance: 30-32 miles one-way
Bike recommendation: Road bike
Essentials: Sunscreen, tool & tire kit, fluorescent jersey, phone
Traffic: Medium
Difficulty: Fairly easy, but round-trip may be a challenge

There's no better road bike ride in all of Northern Michigan than the route along M-22 through the Sleeping Bear National Lakeshore to Glen Arbor.

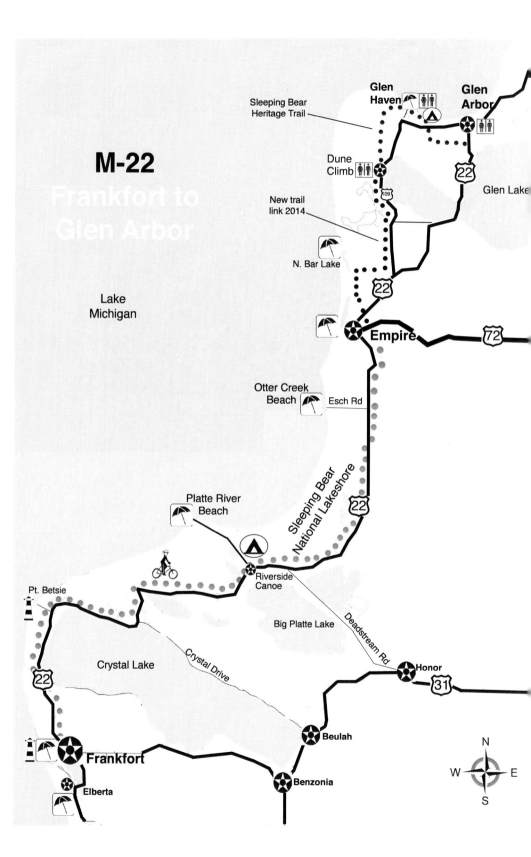

M-22

Frankfort to Glen Arbor

Lake Michigan

Glen Haven

Glen Arbor

Sleeping Bear Heritage Trail

Dune Climb

New trail link 2014

Glen Lake

N. Bar Lake

22

109

22

Empire

72

Otter Creek Beach

Esch Rd

Sleeping Bear National Lakeshore

Platte River Beach

22

Riverside Canoe

Pt. Betsie

Big Platte Lake

Deadstream Rd

Crystal Lake

Crystal Drive

Honor

31

22

Beulah

Frankfort

Elberta

Benzonia

N
W E
S

Bold statement? Yeah, but consider...

Both safety and scenery are factors in making this an outstanding road ride. A broad cycle lane runs the entire distance along M-22 from Frankfort in Benzie County to the national park and Empire where you can catch the new bike path on to Glen Arbor.

Thus, you can ride this route with confidence that you're unlikely to be clipped by a motorist. Long straightaways and gradual downhills also give you a chance to hammer the route if you wish -- it makes for a great speed-work course. There are also a few long climbs along the way to add a smidge of challenge to the route.

WHERE TO BEGIN?

The route is straightforward: just hop on M-22 in Frankfort and head north. At Crystal Lake, you'll come across a mile or so of lakeside homes -- watch out for the driveways. But once you turn the corner into the park you'll be cycling past forests and fields the entire way.

You don't have to start in Frankfort, however; halfway along the route, the **Riverside Canoe** livery at the Platte River crossing also makes a fine starting point. Adjacent to the park's **Platte River Campground**, the livery rents kayaks, canoes and inner tubes for a lazy float down the river and across Loon Lake to a beach on Lake Michigan that's especially popular with families.

Once you hit Empire, take a breather to consider your options. You can either cycle on to Glen Arbor via the Sleeping Bear Heritage Trail, or you can consider a longer ride around the Glen Lakes. See the separate listings for details on these routes and the amenities to be found in Empire and Glen Arbor.

One can, of course, continue riding north from Glen Arbor to Leland and Northport. Be advised, however, that the bike lane alongside M-22 narrows along this stretch and is crumbly and pot-holed in spots. There's also less scenery and more traffic. Leland is about 18 miles north of Glen Arbor with Northport another 11 miles further on.

In total, M-22 runs 116 miles from 3 miles north of Manistee all the way around the Leelanau Peninsula to TC. It's a favorite route of the 9-day Michigan Shoreline Tour which runs 500 miles from New Buffalo at the state line all the way to Mackinaw City. See **http://www.lmb.org** for details.

TC to the Coast
The direct route to Lake Michigan

Distance: 35-plus miles one-way
Bike Recommendation: Hybrid bike
Essentials: Sunscreen, tool & tire kit, fluorescent jersey, phone
Traffic: Light (with one busy stretch of 3-4 miles)
Difficulty: Tough due to many hills & the long ride back to TC

Much of this route is pure bliss, making a beeline for Lake Michigan through the forests of Benzie County along a quiet stretch of Fowler Road.

In fact, this would make an ideal road bike route were it not for the fact of a narrow & nasty 2-3 mile stretch of Cedar Run Road just west of town that tends to be aflame with high-speed traffic. Unfortunately, there's no other feasible option since the paralleling roads have even more traffic.

Thus, it's advisable to ride a hybrid bike on this route, hitting the dirt on the shoulder of the road whenever you hear a car coming. Cedar Run is a commuter route for those living in the sticks west of town and they tend to drive under the delusion that it's a freeway. I assume that many of these drivers are also texting, talking on the phone, or generally not paying attention, and that the last thing they're expecting is a bicycle going down 'their' narrow stretch of pavement.

If you're more of an optimist and prefer the speed of a road bike, you'll find fewer cars on Cedar Run at mid-morning after rush hour. But be sure to wear fluorescent clothing and keep an eye over your shoulder when you hear Mario Andretti, Jr. bearing down on you.

THE ROUTE WEST

It's a cinch to navigate this route, yet relatively few cyclists seem to be familiar with it, since most tend to ride to the coast via Maple City (see the Maple City Run on page 39). Leaving downtown TC, you head west on Front Street past Division for about a half mile. Turn right on Cedar Run Road at **Oleson's Market.** Stay on Cedar Run about a quarter mile and turn right on quiet Barney Road.

There are more than 20 hills along this route, some of them considerable. The biggest of all is Barney Hill, just a half mile out of town. You'll need your highest granny gear to make it up the steep climb on the last 100 yards to the top. But once up Barney (and the lesser monster a mile on) the hills are more manageable.

Continuing down Barney Road, you'll cross Gray Road and carry on a couple of miles until hooking up with Cedar Run again. Take a right and be prepared to endure some traffic for two miles or so, as mentioned above.

Fortunately, the traffic dies down once you get past a few cheapie housing subdivisions. Keep heading west on Cedar Run several miles until it dead-ends on quiet Green Briar Road. Heading left, you'll wind your way around some farmland. Green Briar turns into Fowler Road for a short distance before you take a left at Ole White Drive, continuing on past Mistwood Golf Course and Almira Township Park (rest stop!) to Almira Road (610). Bearing right, you'll pass Maple City Highway (669). Just around the curve is Fowler Road and your straight shot all the way to M-22 and Lake Michigan.

This is where a dense stretch of forests begins and a chance to spot some wildlife.

If you're feeling adventurous and have a hybrid or mountain bike, you can take an alternative two-track route through the woods. Instead of turning left on Ole White Drive, continue down a rough stretch of Fowler past the northern border of Mistwood golf course and across 669. From there, the seasonal road plunges into a deep forest before emerging as the paved version of Fowler heading west.

Once you hit M-22 you're basically in the middle of nowhere. Frankfort lies about 16 miles to the south, while Empire is 6 miles to the north. As noted in the section on riding M-22, there's a broad bike lane heading in both directions and this route is a joy to ride. Enjoy.

Another alternative is to head south to Honor on either Valley Road or Indian Hill Road. From there, you can loop back home via the route described in the "Interlochen to Frankfort" loop on page 73.

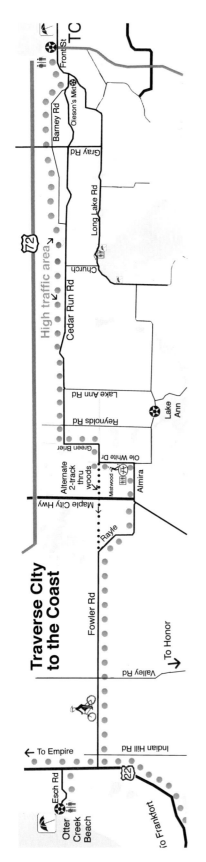

A TOWN CALLED ARAL

Otherwise, a pleasant destination is **Otter Creek Beach**, just to the north of the intersection of Fowler and M-22 on Esch Road. Otter Creek is one of the most beautiful beaches in northwestern lower Michigan and makes for a fine picnic spot or a chance to ease your weary body on the sand.

Back in the lumber era, this was the site of the town of Aral, once a thriving community with a pier and commerce on Lake Michigan.

In 1899, mill owner Charles Wright murdered two Benzie County deputies who were sent to Aral to collect some unpaid taxes, gunning them down on the road that runs across Otter Creek. Wright and his men went back to work as if nothing had happened while the bodies lay in the road, but eventually, he took off and hid in the woods.

A posse of 20 men was organized in the town of Benzonia to bring Wright in. Trying to find Wright's whereabouts, they tortured one of his Ottawa Indian employees, Peter Lahala, by tying a rope around his neck and hoisting him several times into the air from a hanging tree. "Just kick when you're ready to talk," the sheriff said.

Fortunately, Wright was spotted in the woods before Lahala was killed by the posse. Wright was sentenced to a life of hard labor at Jackson Prison.

As for the town of Aral, it became a colony of the House of David cult in the early 1900s under King Ben Purcell. These characters opted for long beards of the ZZ Top variety and loved to play baseball.

They operated a shingle mill here and used the hanging tree for a lighthouse. But eventually, the last of the local timber was cut down and the town disappeared in 1922. Today, there's barely a trace of the old ghost town and Aral lives on as a popular beach destination in the Sleeping Bear National Lakeshore.

Years ago, the stretch of sand to the south of Otter Creek was renowned as Northern Michigan's unofficial gay beach, while nude sunbathers gathered a mile to the north. The nudists, at least, have since been routed by busy-body park rangers.

Around Crystal Lake

Distance: 25 miles
Bike preference: Hybrid or road bike
Essentials: Fluorescent jersey, sunscreen tool, & tire kit
Traffic: Medium
Difficulty: Fairly easy

Cycling around beautiful Crystal Lake has its advantages: in addition to enjoying the cafes and amenities of Frankfort and Beulah, this route takes you down the Betsie Valley Trail.

Crystal Lake is packed with high-priced homes for much of its shoreline, thus the "medium" traffic description. My wife and I always ride the roads with fluorescent yellow vests, and I'd recommend the same for the route around Crystal. Motorists along the lakeshore are courteous in my experience, but there are also many elderly retirees here, so it doesn't hurt to help them see you better.

A LITTLE HISTORY

Some 2,000 years ago, Crystal Lake was a bay of Lake Michigan prior to being enclosed by drifting dunes.

At one time, the lake level was much higher -- perhaps as much as 8-15 feet. Then, in 1873 some local entrepreneurs got the bright idea to create a navigable channel to Lake Michigan. That turned out to be a complete disaster, stranding their boat on dry land and draining the lake to its present level.

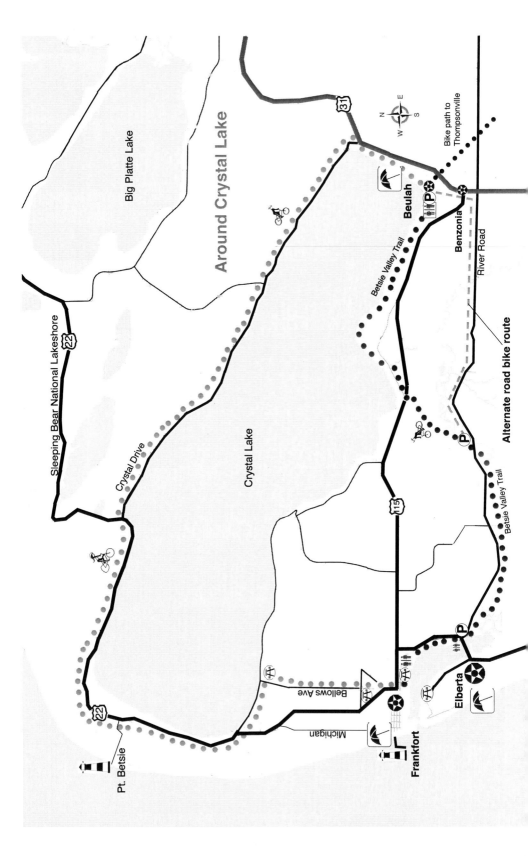

Around Crystal Lake

Big Platte Lake

Sleeping Bear National Lakeshore

Crystal Drive

Crystal Lake

Betsie Valley Trail

Beulah

Benzonia

River Road

Bike path to Thompsonville

N
W   E
S

Alternate road bike route

Betsie Valley Trail

P

P

Elberta

Frankfort

Michigan

Bellows Ave

Pt. Betsie

22

22

31

115

A good thing came of the "Tragedy of Crystal Lake," however, in that the lower water level created the beaches and waterfront for the construction of homes along the shore, including the Village of Beulah. You can still find three monuments to the old lake level along the shore, including at the beach in Beulah.

THE RIDE

Starting in Frankfort, cut right at the park on the north side of town along M-22 and head north on Bellows Avenue. This will take you up and down a steep hill (check your brakes) to the south shore of Crystal Lake. Go left a short distance to M-22 and head right (north).

It's easy-peasy from there on. If lighthouses are your thing, check out Point Betsie -- a well-known landmark.

Continuing north on M-22 you'll turn right on Crystal Drive along the lakeshore. This will take you about three miles past cottages and million-dollar homes to Beulah where you can catch the Betsie Valley Trail at the park in the center of town. See the related description on the BVT to return to Frankfort on page 59.

You can do this route on a road bike if you take care to ride the limestone section of the Betsie Valley Trail. It's a pain in the ass, but I've done it on my road bike by going slow, unclipped, of course.

Otherwise, signs on the trail advise road-bikers to take an alternative route along M-115 to the paved portion of the trail. Bad idea, since the bike lane on 115 is a crumbling, rutted surface with lots of traffic that will have you cussing out the wisdom of this detour. A better option for road-bikers is continuing uphill from Beulah to the Village of Benzonia where you can cycle down quiet River Road a few miles to the hookup with the bike path. Follow the line: ---- on the map for this bypass.

You say you're also into running? Consider the Crystal Lake Team Marathon held in early August. The race can be run solo or as part of a 4-person relay team.

See also: Betsie Valley Trail and Biking M-22.

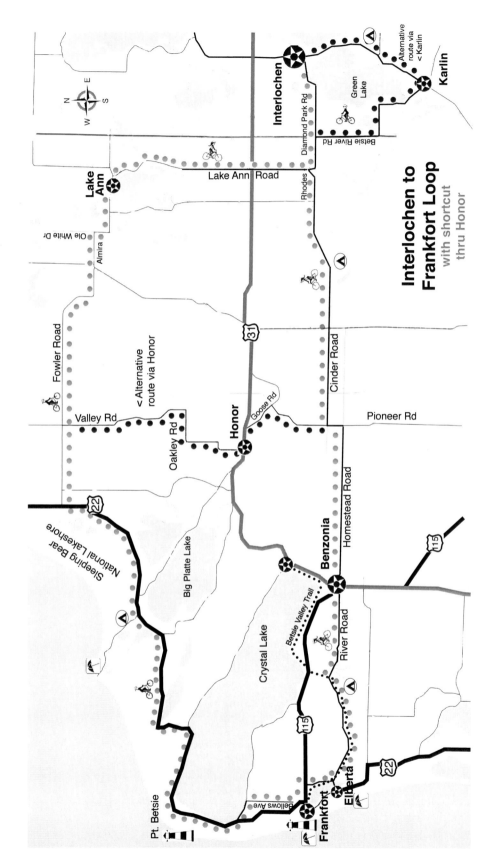

Interlochen to
Frankfort Loop
with shortcut
thru Honor

Interlochen to Frankfort Loop

Distance: About 75 miles
Bike Recommendation: Road bike or hybrid
Essentials: fluorescent jersey, tool & tire kit, phone, sunscreen.
Traffic: Light to medium
Difficulty: Tough, because of distance & hills

This scenic loop route offers a 'back way' to Frankfort through Benzie County with relatively light traffic. The return route takes you north on M-22 and then east along a quiet country road to Lake Ann and back to Interlochen.

With its many restaurants, beach and pier, Frankfort makes a superb destination for this day-trip ride. Why not break it up and spend the night? Heading back, you'll pedal along the shores of beautiful Crystal Lake and through part of the Sleeping Bear National Lakeshore.

Years ago, this was part of my favorite century ride out of Traverse City -- but more on that later.

WEST TO FRANKFORT

Departing from the north end of the Interlochen Arts Academy Campus, you can either head west along Diamond Park Road past the cottages along Green Lake or head south a couple of miles to the crossroads of Karlin for a slightly more scenic route.

Either way, you'll be heading for Betsie River Road which takes you north to Cinder Road.

Take a left on Cinder Road and ride west past Thompsonville Highway to S. Zimmerman Road and take a left (south). When you reach Homestead Road, take a right and head west past Benzie Central High School.

Note: Homestead Road offers the most traffic you're likely to encounter on the way to Frankfort and it's a relatively narrow road that lends itself to speeding cars. Keep an eye over your shoulder along this stretch which is, mercifully, relatively short.

Soon, you'll come to a very steep hill just before the village of Benzonia. Take it slow on this downhill because there's a stop sign at the bottom and you have no way of knowing if you'll get nailed at the blind intersection by a motorist.

Crossing 115 in Benzonia (near the excellent **Roadhouse** Mexican restaurant), you head several miles down River Road until it

connects to the Betsie Valley Trailway just after the river. You can ride the bike trail all the way into Frankfort.

THE RETURN ROUTE

Heading north out of Frankfort on the bike shoulder along M-22 you'll pass Crystal Lake and head into Sleeping Bear National Lakeshore. Several miles to the north you'll pass Riverside Canoe livery on the Platte River, then Deadstream Road. Keep going.

When you reach Fowler Road, take a right and head east along this quiet country road through the forest. You'll loop around to the left to Almira Road at the end of Fowler and continue on for a mile to Ole White Drive. Take a right and head south into the village of Lake Ann.

Once through the village, take a right on Lake Ann Road (665) and head south, crossing US 31. This will curve east, turning into Rhodes Road, which turns into Diamond Park Road, taking you back to Interlochen.

A CENTURY ROUTE

It's possible to expand this route as a century ride by riding to Interlochen from Traverse City. Parking at West Senior High School on North Long Lake Road, you bike south along quiet Herkner Road and East and South Long Lake Roads to Interlochen, heading on to Frankfort. From there, you cycle back to TC via the Fowler Road route (see TC to the Coast, page 66).

Although there's a narrow bike lane along Long Lake Road, it's also true that traffic from TC to Interlochen has increased considerably through the years. If possible, rise early and hustle along that stretch of South Long Lake Road before the traffic starts.

As a final caution, it may be tempting to ride the wide shoulder of US 31 part of the way to Frankfort, but be aware that much of the heavy traffic along this route is moving at 60 mph or more, and the shoulder of the road is cracked and potholed in spots.

See also: Riding M-22, Around Crystal Lake, and Traverse City to Otter Creek for refinements of this route.

Notes:

Antrim County

It's not hard to get lost in Antrim County, which offers some of the largest -- and most sinuous -- inland lakes in the region, including Elk Lake, Torch Lake and Lake Bellaire, all requiring a tangle of roads to get around them.

For cyclists, "getting lost" can offer some pleasant options once you've wheeled your way to say, **Short's Brewing** in Bellaire, or the beach town charm of Elk Rapids with its many restaurants, art galleries and boutiques.

Don't Miss:

- TC to Elk Rapids
- The Ride Around Torch Lake

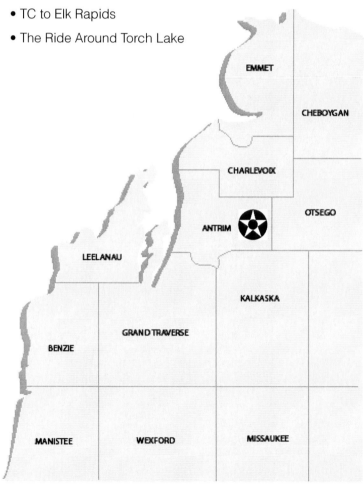

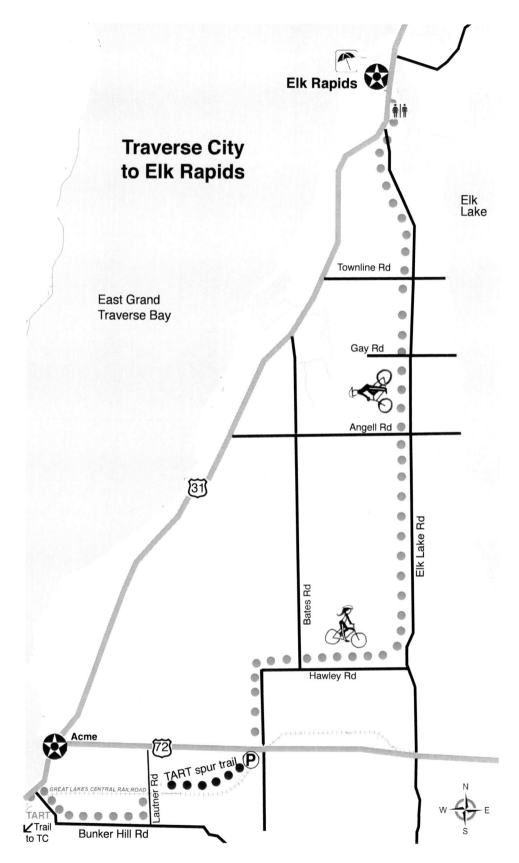

TC to Elk Rapids

Distance: About 15 miles one-way
Bike recommendation: Road bike
Essentials: fluorescent jersey, tool & tire kit, phone
Traffic: Light
Difficulty: Fairly easy -- a few hills

Elk Rapids is the closest beach town to Traverse City and a good lunch or dinner destination if you're up for a road bike ride.

Forget riding up US-31 with its heavy traffic; there's a quiet route up the 'back way' along Elk Lake Road (605) that takes you over rolling hills with superb vistas of the surrounding farms and orchards.

For starters, you'll want to ride from TC to the eastern end of the TART Trail in Acme. Head up Bunker Hill Road a mile or so and take a left on Lautner Road. Less than half-mile on, you'll find a little-known satellite TART Trail which takes you to Williamsburg and M-72.

Crossing M-72, head north along S. Bates Road. Head right on Brackett/Hawley and proceed to Elk Lake Road. It's a straight shot from there north to Elk Rapids.

For a quick lunch, check out **Chef Charles Pizza** downtown on River Street, an Elk Rapids institution. Heartier appetites will appreciate the **Harbor Cafe.** A can't-miss is the **Sweet Shop**, one of the finest bakeries in Northern Michigan. To rub elbows with locals, check out **Java Jones**, the big coffeehouse hangout in ER.

Be sure to check out the town's **library** -- it's perched atop a tiny island just off the marina. And if you're feeling 'just beachy,' Elk Rapids can accommodate with a stretch of sand facing East Grand Traverse Bay.

Elk Rapids is also the launching point for the **Ride Around Torch** bike tour which takes place in mid July. Check out the next section on cycling Torch Lake if you'd like to be part of the action.

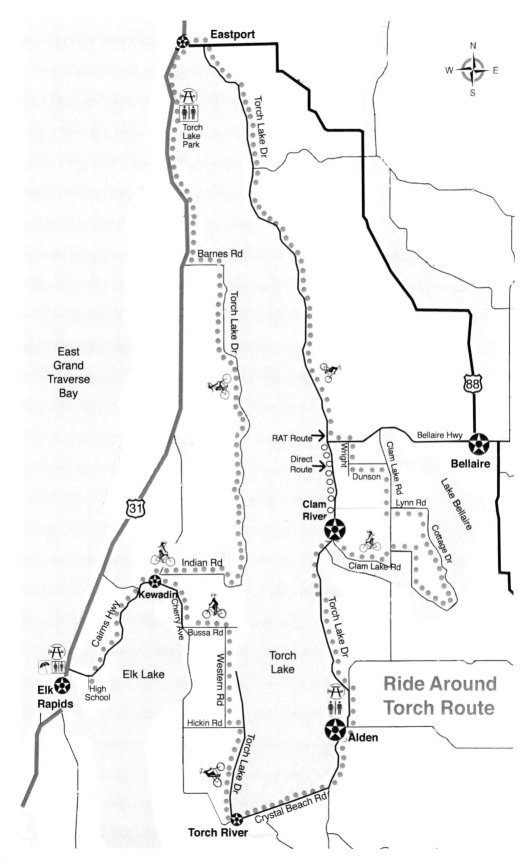

Around Torch Lake

Distance: 55-63 miles
Bike recommendation: Road bike or hybrid
Essentials: Sunscreen, fluorescent jersey, tool & tire kit, phone
Traffic: Light to medium
Difficulty: Tough because of distance & hills at end of route

There are two ways to ride around Torch Lake: either go it alone on a blissful ride with a friend, or hook up with 1,200 cycle buddies for the annual **Ride Around Torch (RAT)** bike tour in mid July.

Both options have their benefits. The 63-mile route described here follows the RAT from the town of Elk Rapids around the lake and back.

Torch Lake got its name from the Ojibwa, who called it Was-wa-gon-ong -- "Place of the Torches." Here, native fishermen used torches at night to spear fish or catch them in nets. It's said that the first white settlers called it "Torch Light Lake."

At 19 miles in length, Torch is the longest inland lake in Michigan and second in size only to Houghton Lake. Like Glen Lake in Leelanau County, it makes the claim of being one of the top 10 most beautiful lakes in the world, as touted by *National Geographic*. Dispute this to any lake resident and you've just thrown down some fightin' words.

Unfortunately, this legendary beauty is well-veiled from passing cyclists by the homes of the wealthy and cottage owners. You barely get a glimpse of the lake along the entire ride.

Those who do enjoy its views, however, include a list of celebrity homeowners. Filmmaker Michael Moore had a timber frame mansion built here in the late '00s. Local gossip has it that other celebs with second homes here include Eminem, Kid Rock, Dave Mathews, Tigers pitcher Kirk Gibson, attorney Geoffrey Fieger and actresses Christine Lahti and Julie Kavner, among others. Some of these folks probably never actually lived on Torch, and some may have moved on. Online, for instance, the same mansion is pictured as the residence of Moore, Kid Rock and Eminem... strange bedfellows, if true.

HEADING NORTH

Although the route curves around here and there, you're likely to find the arrows of last year's RAT to serve as a guide. Just be sure you don't get sidetracked down the RAT's 100-mile loop which packs lots of hills.

Parking at Elk Rapids High School just off Ames Street at Third Street on the northeast side of town, you head east on Cairns Highway. This stretch is likely to be the most traffic you'll encounter on the ride. Take Indian Road to Torch Lake Drive and head north for most of the length of the lake to Barnes Road where you'll cut west for a couple of miles riding on US 31-North. Fortunately, there's a broad shoulder here to accommodate cyclists, but be sure to stay far to the right as traffic tends to run 60mph or more.

Just past Eastport you turn right on highway 88, passing a former tavern which once hosted rock stars traveling to and from the Castle Farms' music venue in the '80s. Sometimes is seems like half the boozers in Northern Michigan can recall the time they shared a beer and a game of darts with Rod Stewart at this place.

ROUND THE BEND

Heading south on Torch Lake Drive, you'll have a languorous ride down the lakeshore. The RAT route makes a detour to the east on Bellaire Highway, passing by Bellaire Lake and Clam Lake. This is so riders can get in their 100k bragging rights. If that's not a concern, you can cut off about 7-8 miles by continuing down Torch Lake Drive (593) to the Village of Alden.

The Alden Bar makes a great stop for lunch, offering burgers and other bar food. Along with **Short's Brewing** in Bellaire, it's one of the most happening places in Antrim County with a music scene at night and locals rubbing elbows with tourists.

At the bottom of the lake, you cross Torch River just off the site of the **Torch Lake Sandbar**, which is a cause for considerable aggravation by lakeshore residents. This is the sandbar made legend by Kid Rock in his song, "All Summer Long." Hundreds of drunken boaters and kids party on the sandbar through the summer, exhibiting the same kind of "show us your boobs!" spirit that you'd expect from the Mardi Gras. The *Northern Express Weekly* dubbed it "Torch Lake Babylon."

The last stretch of the ride is the toughest, taking you north over a series of hills inland and around Elk Lake back to Elk Rapids. Be sure to save some water, or perhaps some energy from that beer you had back in Alden for this stretch.

RIDING THE RAT

Want company? For biking camaraderie it's hard to beat the RAT, which is one of Northern Michigan's top bike tours, hosted by the Cherry Capital Cycling Club.

The RAT falls on the third Sunday in July, offering 26, 63 and 100 mile loops with a maximum of 1,200 riders. There are several refreshment stops along the route, a sag wagon to help those in a jam, and a big picnic on the beach at the end.

If you ride the RAT, be sure to get an early start. It can get really hot on the last hilly stretch around the lake, and in any event, you'll want to arrive at the picnic early enough to chat with your fellow bikies. This can't be stressed enough: I've known a number of riders who got a late start and deeply regretted both the afternoon heat and missing out on the party.

Web: http://www.cherrycapitalcyclingclub.org

Notes:

Little Traverse

The Little Traverse area -- including Charlevoix and Emmet counties -- easily rivals Grand Traverse as a cycling destination. Since its formation in 1995 the Top of Michigan Trails Council in Petoskey has assisted in the creation of an amazing 288 miles of trails that ramble far beyond the Little Traverse area.

It's possible to ride all the way from Charlevoix to Mackinaw City on a network of trails. The region is also noteworthy for the famed "Tunnel of Trees" route north of Harbor Springs. And one couldn't ask for finer amenities in the form of restaurants, shops and cycle stores than those found in downtown Petoskey which serves as the heart of the region.

Don't Miss:

- The Wheelway

- Petoskey to Alanson

- Beaver Island

- Around Lake Charlevoix

- Around Walloon Lake

- The Tunnel of Trees

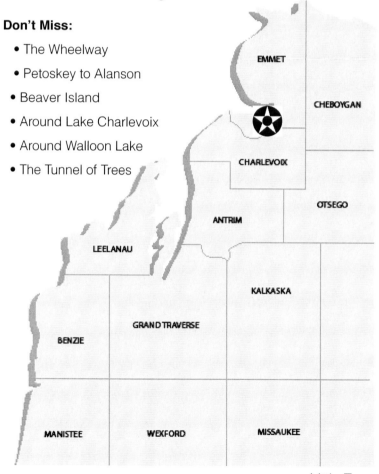

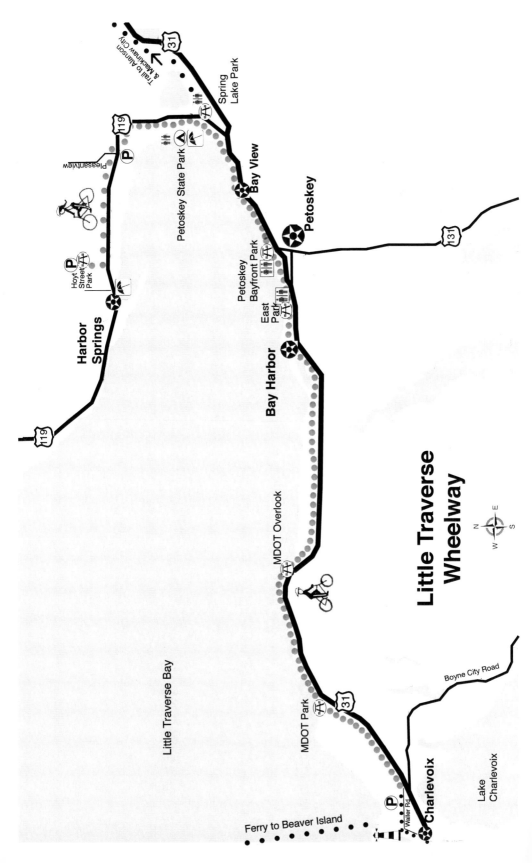

The Wheelway: Charlevoix to Harbor Springs

Distance: 26 miles
Bike recommendation: All good
Essentials: Sunscreen, windbreaker, tool & tire kit, energy foods
Traffic: None
Difficulty: Easy

Oh, how the motorists driving between Charlevoix and Petoskey on US 31 must envy the cyclists on the path by the roadway. This is one of Northern Michigan's most scenic trail rides with sparkling views of Lake Michigan and Little Traverse Bay.

Bonus: this ride takes you past the ritzy environs of Bay Harbor, where you can stop for some pancakes or a beer and speculate on what life is like for those who can afford to park their yachts in their basement boathouses.

"The Wheelway Trail from Harbor Springs to Charlevoix is just exploding with cyclists," said Jeff Winegard, executive director of the **Top of Michigan Trails Council** in Petoskey, in a 2012 interview with *Northern Express Weekly*. "We think a lot of people are coming to Northern Michigan these days just to use the Wheelway."

The Trails Council is justifiably proud of its achievements: it spearheaded the Wheelway project and has assisted in the creation of 288 miles of trails in the region since its formation in 1995.

ROLLING NORTH

Easy to find near the **Charlevoix Community Pool** at the north end of town, you can park at the nearby township hall which is located one-half mile down adjacent Waller Road.

Soon you come across a boardwalk which runs for more than half a mile along the roadway. A screen of trees offers some relief from the adjacent traffic as you head north.

Big Rock Point lies a short way north of Charlevoix. Once, this was the site of Michigan's first nuclear power plant and the fifth in the nation -- a big, blue gum ball with a candy cane smokestack parked on the shores of Lake Michigan.

The plant operated between 1962 and 1997, boiling water from Lake Michigan to produce the steam that drove its turbines,

The only bicycle tunnel in Northern Michigan is located west of Bay Harbor's Village.

generating 67 megawatts of electricity. Although the plant was a pipsqueak by today's standards, it's also true that a single 10-ton shot of uranium could produce as much electricity as 260,000 tons of coal.

Incredibly, the nuclear power plant was a tourist attraction from 1961-1970 with hundreds of thousands of visitors welcomed by a video of future president Ronald Reagan, who was then a spokesman for General Electric. As a child, I recall our family touring the plant. The cartoon character Reddy Kilowatt informed us that we were on the threshold of a wonderful new age of limitless nuclear power which would unleash "the mighty atom." It seemed the Jetsons era of flying cars and robot dogs was just around the corner.

For 11 years, the plant produced Cobalt 60 as a byproduct, used in the treatment of cancer patients. It's estimated the material saved 120,000 lives.

But things went sour for Big Rock, with anti-nuclear activists from the Little Traverse area demanding its closure throughout the '80s and '90s.

It cost $390 million to decommission the plant, tear it down and ship its components to waste dumps. Today, Big Rock Point is a Nuclear Historic Landmark and there's a mini shrine to the plant alongside the Wheelway which offers its history in detail, omitting any word of the protests. Ironically, environmentalists are now reconsidering nuclear power as an alternative to the hazards of fossil fuel and global warming.

Just north of Big Rock you'll find a picnic area that offers fine views of the lake. Nearby is the **Northern Lake Michigan Spiritualist Camp**, one of America's more imaginative religious endeavors. A popular movement in the late 1800s and early 1900s, spiritualism aims to communicate with the dead. The movement got its start in March, 1848 when the Fox family managed to communicate with the murdered spirit of one Charles B. Rosna.

BUBBLE, BUBBLE...

... toil & trouble. That was the downside of the development miracle of **Bay Harbor** which lies a few miles further on.

For over 100 years, this 5-mile stretch of lakeshore served as a gravel mining and cement plant operation spread across 1,200 acres. When the plant shut down in the 1980s, it left behind a desert of 2.5-million cubic yards of kiln dust, laden with poisons such as chromium, asbestos and mercury.

Inexplicably, the Michigan DNR certified this wasteland as inert -- mere dirt, it seemed -- and in 1993, developer David V. Johnson teamed up with CMS Energy to begin work on the Bay Harbor luxury resort town. Within seven years, a second city had been constructed south of Petoskey that featured a luxury hotel, the homes of the super rich (Madonna was said to own one), the **Bay Harbor Equestrian Club** and a 27-hole golf course -- the "Pebble Beach of the Midwest."

Johnson had an interesting background. Coming from working class roots in the Detroit area, he showed early promise as a businessman in college at Michigan State University, leasing seven gas stations in East Lansing. He earned a B.S. in packaging engineering and went on to become a luxury home real estate developer in the Bloomfield Hills area of Detroit. In 1978, he broke his neck in a swimming pool accident, but even partial paralysis didn't keep him from realizing his ambitions.

Fortunately for him, Johnson signed a do-not-sue covenant with the DNR, which was common with toxic waste cleanup sites, along with another agreement that CMS Energy would take the legal responsibility if anything went tits-up with the project. It did: the kiln dust beneath Bay Harbor soon revealed itself to be packed with toxic compounds. When water filtered through the dust it created a leachate filled with heavy metals, including lead, arsenic and mercury. The leachate burned like bleach, even searing the skin of those swimming in the bay. The resulting mess (and uproar) necessitated hundreds of millions in clean-up costs.

But don't let that stop you from enjoying breakfast at the popular **Original Pancake House** or a drink at **Knot Just a Bar** on the waterfront.

DOWNTOWN PETOSKEY

Rolling on, you'll come to the spectacular views of **East Park** -- a great place for a picnic and a chance snap a 'selfie' with the opulent hotel at Bay Harbor in the background. About two miles on you reach downtown Petoskey, where the Bayfront Park with the former railroad station (now a museum) makes for a good place to lock your bike while strolling around town. The **Little Traverse History Museum** notes that this stretch of waterfront boasted the very first bike path in Northern Michigan, established in the late 1880s when newfangled bicycles were all the rage with resorters pouring in on steamers from Detroit and Chicago.

The streets of downtown Petoskey can occupy an afternoon, with art galleries along the Gaslight District, two bookstores, Pennsylvania Park, the **Grain Train** coop and other attractions. One of the most popular hangouts in town is **Roast & Toast** on Lake Street a coffeeshop and cafe which offers light dining options.

Take a seat at the bar of the **City Park Grill** and you'll find yourself at the same spot where young Ernest Hemingway wrote some of the Nick Adams stories. These rough tales of Northern Michigan enthralled the literati of Paris in the 1920s, leading to Hemingway's coronation as the Greatest Writer in the World.

Back then, this place was known as the Grill Cafè, not far from the boarding house where Hemingway lived in 1919 at the age of 20. He was just back from World War I, recovering from leg wounds suffered during his stint as an ambulance driver on the Italian front. Legend has it that a tunnel under the bar led to the local brothel. Good luck finding it today.

Moving on, you'll come to the historic **Bay View** neighborhood of grand old Victorian homes, a colony once inspired by the Chautauqua movement of the 19th century. Salons emphasizing enlightened conversation, the arts and guest speakers invigorated the neighborhood back when, and still do to this day.

TO HARBOR SPRINGS

The bike path through Petoskey bypasses a snarl of traffic along US 31, which streams down a roadway fit for a pinball game. Near the intersection of US 31 and 119 you'll find a gallery specializing in Native American crafts and artwork as well as the towering **Petoskey Brewing**, a microbrewery which has re-occupied a long-shuttered establishment. At Spring Lake Park you'll find the turnoff for the new bike trail to Alanson.

Need a swim? **Petoskey State Park** is the place to beach it. From here, you continue north on the bike path which crosses 119 at Pleasantview Road, 4 miles east of Harbor Springs for a pleasant roll into town. You'll find trailhead parking at the baseball field on the corner of Hoyt and Lake streets at Park Lane in Harbor Springs.

Web: www.trails council.org

Petoskey to Alanson

Distance: 7.5 miles
Bike recommendation: All good
Essentials: Money for ice cream
Traffic: None
Difficulty: Easy

In some ways, the new bike path from Petoskey to Alanson bears similarities to the Leelanau Trail out of Traverse City.

Both trails take riders from the hustle and traffic of Northern Michigan's largest cities to natural surroundings in a matter of minutes. And both end in up-and-coming communities which are happy to receive the largesse of visiting cyclists.

Established in 2013, the trailhead for the new bike path is at

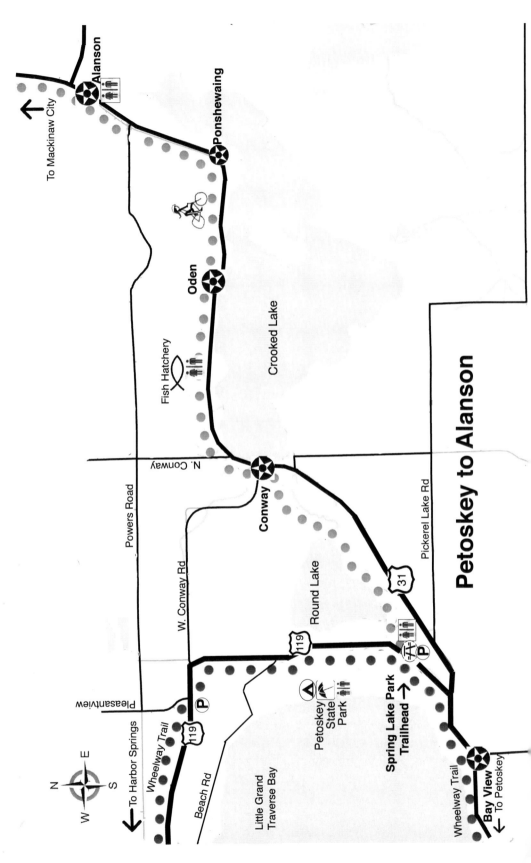

Petoskey to Alanson

Alanson
To Mackinaw City
Ponshewaing
Oden
Fish Hatchery
Crooked Lake
Powers Road
N. Conway
Conway
W. Conway Rd
Round Lake
Pickerel Lake Rd
31
119
Pleasantview
To Harbor Springs
Wheelway Trail
119
Beach Rd
Little Grand Traverse Bay
Petoskey State Park
Spring Lake Park Trailhead →
Wheelway Trail
Bay View
To Petoskey

N
E
S
W

Spring Lake Park on US 119, conveniently located midway between Petoskey and Harbor Springs off the Wheelway Trail.

The trail wanders through a nature area south of Round Lake where you'll be serenaded by an orchestra of songbirds and spring peepers.

Pedaling north, the trail skirts Crooked Lake. Don't miss the Oden State Fish Hatchery Visitor Center along this stretch, which includes a nature trail and several ponds, including one stocked with large trout basking in the sun. Visitors can feed the fish used to restock Michigan's lakes and rivers. Displays include a 1914-1935 Wolverine train car which once transported the fish keepers of the old Michigan Department of Conservation around the state on their fish-stocking mission.

The trail runs along busy highway 31 thereafter, which is a bit of a buzzkill, but it beats riding on the highway shoulder and you quickly find yourself in Alanson.

This old lumber town is on the rebound from years of decline and now sports a number of new businesses. In the mid '90s, the town was in the world spotlight for several years as being the home of Norm Olson, who headquartered the Northern Michigan Regional Militia out of the tiny Alanson Armory gun shop in his home. Olson reportedly moved on to Alaska several years ago.

There are a number of restaurants and watering holes in town with the most picturesque being the **Alanson Depot** which is housed in a former train station that dates back to the 1880s. The restaurant's menu notes that after the surrounding forests were depleted of lumber the railway line got into the tourist business, bringing downstaters to the communities of Alanson, Topinabee and Bay View on a train called "The Fishing Line." Tourists have been on their way "Up North" ever since.

As you ride this trail, you might reflect that tragedy can strike even on a bike path. A cyclist from Petoskey was biking the new trail in July, 2013 before it was marked with stop signs and officially opened; he rolled through an unmarked intersection at the South Luce Street in Oden and was struck and killed by a car.

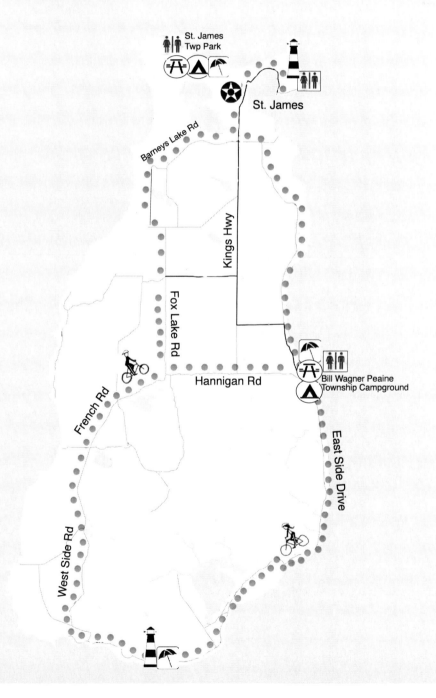

Garden Island

Beaver Island

St. James Twp Park

St. James

Barneys Lake Rd

Kings Hwy

Fox Lake Rd

French Rd

Hannigan Rd

Bill Wagner Peaine Township Campground

West Side Rd

East Side Drive

Beaver Island

Distance: 20-40 miles
Bike recommendation: Mountain bike or hybrid
Essentials: Dust mask, extra water, energy foods, swim suit, tool & tire kit, sunscreen
Traffic: Light
Difficulty: Can be tough, due to poor road conditions

When you take the 32-mile trip by ferry from Charlevoix to Beaver Island, consider that the Indians made this trip as long as 2,200 years ago in their frail birch bark canoes.

The waves can come up fast and high on Lake Michigan -- like 8-10 feet or more -- and today, few sailors make the trip in anything less than a 30-foot boat. Yet the Chippewa and Ottawa established villages on the island archipelago around Beaver Island, particularly on Garden Island which is just to the north. Some were fleeing the encroachment of white settlers.

Still alive with the currents of history, Beaver Island may not be the most fun you've ever had on a bike, but you'll come away feeling you've had an experience like nothing else in North America.

SOUTHERN LOOP

You can rent bikes on the island, but a better option is simply to bring your own on the ferry.

The ride is a no-brainer. Just head south from the Village of St. James, enjoying a few miles of pavement on Kings Highway. This turns into East Side Drive, and then it's gravel & dirt roads all the way around the island and back.

Beaver Island runs 13 miles long and 3-6 miles wide and is mostly forest and swamps in the interior with not much to see other than one heck of a lot of rabbits. The entire way around is about 40 miles -- a long haul on dirt roads, so you may wish to ride a shorter loop. Explore and enjoy.

Also, be sure to pack a handkerchief or something to use as a dust mask -- you'll need it, cowboy, unless a recent rain has dampened the sandy roads. Two water bottles? Yup, at least.

If you're into cycle camping, the **Bill Wagner Peaine Township Campground** located 7 miles south of town offers 22 rustic campsites. Bear in mind there are no showers and only pit toilets, but you will enjoy fabulous views of the Mackinac Bridge lit up at night, and the spectrum of the Milky Way at its fullest intensity. A group of friends and I ditched our tents to sleep on the beach on our bike trip here, waking covered with dew at dawn, but exhilarated by the stellar light show.

There's also **St. James Township Campground** just a mile north of town with 12 sites overlooking

The southern tip of Beaver Island.

Garden Island. Otherwise, there are several inns and B&B options in town.

The main destination for cyclists is the **Head Light** and beach at the south end of the island. This lighthouse was first constructed in 1858 to help passing ships navigate the tricky channel between the island and Gray's Reef. In 1975, the keeper's quarters was acquired by Charlevoix Public Schools for $1 and an alternative school for students ages 16-21 was established in 1978.

The lighthouse makes for a pleasant beach break and picnic stop. Thereafter, you can either ride back the way you came, or continue on along heavily wooded French Bay Road which turns into West Side Road and then Fox Lake Road back to St. James.

KING STRANG

Today, evidence of the Irish settlers of Beaver Island is everywhere. The fishermen of Donegal and mainland Ireland found this remote corner of the Old Northwest to be much like home and sank deep Catholic roots here. For decades, Gaelic was spoken on the island, and there are still many reminders of Irish influence, including the popular **Shamrock Restaurant and Pub**. Wander through the old cemetery just out of town and you'll find poignant tales of love and loss amid its crumbling tombstones.

Before the Irish, however, Beaver Island was the wished-for utopia of Mormon King James Strang and his followers, who set out to establish an American Zion here in 1848.

When Mormon founder Joseph Smith was hauled out of jail in Carthage, Illinois and killed by a mob in 1844, many of his followers headed west with Brigham Young to Utah. But some followed Strang to Beaver Island, establishing a colony of Strangites.

King Strang was a moralizing hypocrite who had 5 wives (some say 6-7) and 14 kids. Elected to the Michigan Legislature in 1853 and 1855, he did much to shape the governance of Northern Michigan and established its first newspaper. But he was dictatorial and self-righteous about what his followers could or couldn't do, and also bullied non-Mormon residents of the island.

Bad blood between the Mormons and non-believers boiled over into fights and confrontations. In one incident, a boatload of Mormons was attacked and shot at by fishermen from what was then called Fish Town (Charlevoix), who moonlighted as pirates.

King Strang's rule lasted just 8 years, ending with his death in 1856. When two women refused to follow his fundamentalist dress code, he had their husbands flogged and publicly humiliated. The men took their revenge by shooting him in the back as he was walking aboard the USS Michigan for a tour of the war ship which guarded the Great Lakes. His murderers fled on the ship to Mackinac Island and were never charged -- a sign perhaps, of the non-believer's aversion for King Strang.

Mobs of armed men from Mackinac and St. Helena islands stormed the Mormon colony of 2,600 people and drove them from their homes. A lawless community took root with anarchy being the order of the day until the State intervened in 1877.

BIKE FEST

If you like company, the annual **Beaver Island Bike Festival** is held on the third weekend in June, hosted by **North Country Cycle Sport** out of Boyne City and Petoskey.

The Bike Fest offers 40 and 20-mile loops with parties and a BBQ bash with live music at the Shamrock among other amenities running through the weekend. See the website for details.

http://beaverislandbikefestival.com

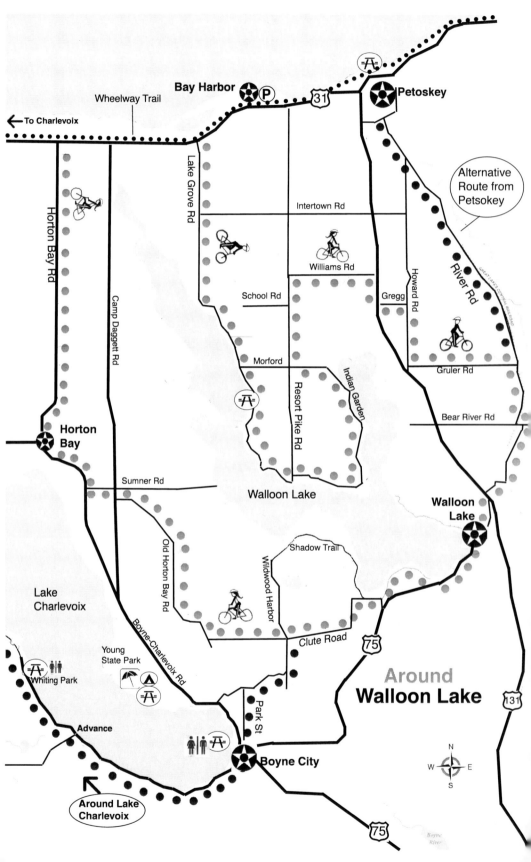

Around Walloon Lake

Distance: 43 miles
Bike recommendation: Road bike
Essentials: fluorescent jersey, extra water, energy foods, tool & tire kit, sunscreen, windbreaker
Traffic: Light to medium -- very busy on short 131 link
Difficulty: Semi tough -- because of hills & distance

Walloon Lake is steeped in the history of the Little Traverse area. In addition to being the boyhood getaway of Ernest Hemingway, whose family vacationed up here each summer from Oak Park near Chicago, the lake boomed during the resort era of the late 1800s - early 1900s.

Back then, resorters from downstate and Chicago flocked to Petoskey via huge steamships as well as on the "Fishing Line" railway. They were ferried to their homes around the lake on the Steamship Tourist. During the evening, they were often enthralled by the Chautauqua-style lectures and concerts in nearby Bay View.

THE RIDE

Cycling around the lake has its pleasures, but also some challenges. There are a few big hills along the route, a bit of traffic to avoid here and there, and many twists and turns.

These challenges are chiefly due to the need to avoid the north-south traffic heading to and from the residential areas south of Petoskey.

But it is possible to find some quiet roads around the lake and to pull off a 40-plus mile loop from Petoskey.

Speaking of which, although it may be tempting to start in Petoskey by heading down River Road, a better option is to begin your ride in Bay Harbor so you don't miss the best views of Walloon Lake. These can be found at the end of quiet Lake Grove Road, which turns into Indian Garden Road at the base of the peninsula.

Gentle hills rolling through forests carpeted with trilliums give way to the best views of Walloon Lake that you'll find on the route. Here too are a clutch of posh homes of the sort that provide eye candy for *Traverse the Magazine*. These boondock palazzos range from new timber frames and log homes to resort-era 'cottages' from Hemingway's day.

Once your home tour is over, get down to business scrambling north on Resort Pike as fast as possible. There's a narrow bike path here, but a fair amount of traffic too. Unfortunately, you also have to ride the shoulder of busy highway 131 a bit further on, but for less than half a mile.

Thereafter, it's a pleasant ride down River Road, curving around to the village of Walloon Lake and a park which makes for a good rest stop. Here, you have the aggravation of riding the rough bike lane alongside busy route 75, fortunately not for long. That gives way to a network of country roads leading you to Horton Bay Road and back home.

You wouldn't think that a route around a lake would have many hills. Guess again -- there's an especially high ridge to cross on Horton Bay Road along with numerous smaller hills much of the way around this route. If you're into hill training, consider this your lucky day.

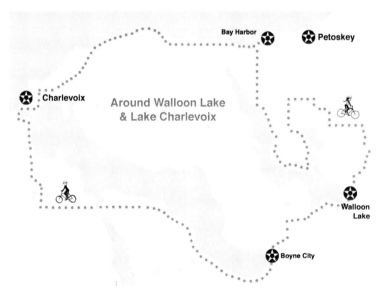

THE BIG LOOP: You can combine the routes around Walloon Lake and Lake Charlevoix for a great 62-mile ride. This route also cuts off the problematical hill on Horton Bay Road and provides a pleasant ride down The Wheelway. The two routes link up off Clute Road, just north of Boyne City.

Around Lake Charlevoix

Distance: 43 miles
Bike recommendation: Road bike
Essentials: Energy foods, tool & tire kit, sunscreen, windbreaker, fluorescent jersey
Traffic: Light to medium
Difficulty: Semi tough -- because of distance

A cyclist can't look at a map of the Little Traverse region without fantasizing about riding around Lake Charlevoix -- it just begs to be ridden.

And indeed, this loop offers a tantalizing mix for cyclists. The route includes a ride on the legendary Ironton ferry along with stops in Horton Bay, Boyne City, and of course, Charlevoix.

But slow down, cowpoke, because this ride isn't as straightforward as it looks. Although the Boyne City-Charlevoix Road has been improved and widened on the north shore of the lake, many local cyclists prefer to skip this leg because of its high-speed traffic. There's a bike lane on the highway, but it's a narrow one, and at any rate, there's not much to see on this road.

Currently, the Top of Michigan Trails Council is working with local governments to construct a new bike path that will link Boyne City and Charlevoix. But in the meantime, consider bypassing the north shore of the lake for the much more scenic route along the Wheelway Bikepath which runs along the shore of sparkling Lake Michigan.

THE NORTH SHORE

Starting at the Wheelway Trailhead (you can park at the Charlevoix Pool or the nearby township hall on Waller Road), head east past Big Rock Point. About a mile before the main entrance to Bay Harbor (another possible starting point), you'll come to Horton Bay Road. Head south.

Horton Bay Road is less than ideal, but it's the lesser of two evils, the other being the parallel Camp Daggett Road. Both are

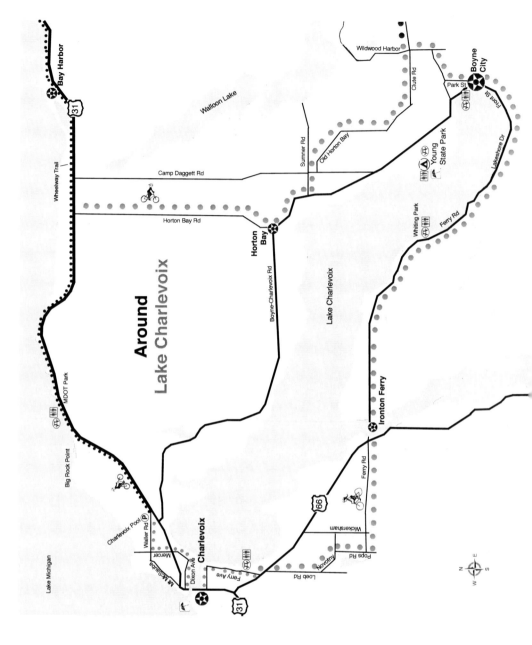

quite hilly and narrow. Yet although Horton Bay Road is considered a truck route, it seems to have less traffic and there's a bike lane on the southern third of its length.

Both roads have an absolute monster of a hill past the halfway point which will have you cursing me and this book for suggesting this route. But, it is what it is, owing to the huge ridges around Petoskey which were created at the end of the last Ice Age.

Once you make it down this one tough stretch you will be rewarded with a visit to the old-timey **Horton Bay General Store**. Once upon a time, young Ernie Hemingway sat on the porch of this store, spooning with his girl Becky Thatcher over cherry fizzes. Oh wait, Becky was Tom Sawyer's girlfriend; whatever the case, young Hemingway surely must have kissed some local gal here during his teen years in the area, or at least bought some candy.

Traveling down nearby Sumner Road, you head the back way in to Boyne City. This town is renowned for its excellent dining options, including the regionally-famous **Red Mesa Grill**, which offers South of the Border and Central American specialties. Personally, I opted for the bare bones **Bob's Spicy Pizza** joint with its pathetic hand-lettered sign just north of town because it offered a chance to gulp down a meatball sub while keeping an eye on my bike.

BELIEVE IT

The route from here on offers great views of the lake (and a touch of its chilly winds) all the way to the Ironton ferry. Here, for $1, you can cross over the south arm of Lake Charlevoix on a run that it made "Ripley's Believe It Or Not" decades ago. A plaque from the book notes that the ferry had traveled 15,000 miles while never venturing more than 1,000 feet from its port.

It's rolling farmland the rest of the back way into Charlevoix. Once on Ferry Ave., you'll find a row of eye-popping mansions, the likes of which you'd think only a mafioso chieftain or English lord could afford. Mutter a prayer of thanks that you don't have their heating bills as you roll into downtown.

Here, it's every man or woman to him/herself because Charlevoix is well known as being the worst traffic bottleneck in Northern Michigan. Since the many tourists traveling through are likely to be gawking everywhere but the road, you may want to walk your bike through town.

Once past the drawbridge, take an immediate right on Dixon and a left on Mercer to get back to Waller Road and the bike path.

Dining options in Charlevoix include **The Villager Pub** downtown, which is highly regarded for its affordable whitefish. Another good choice is **Kelsey B's** back on Ferry Ave. which offers a maritime theme in a sprawling restaurant overlooking the lake. Ditto **Stafford's Weathervane**, a hobbit-style spread above the drawbridge. For coffee and deli sandwiches or salads, check out **Scovie's Gourmet** which is also near the bridge.

Notes:

The Mackinac Straits
5 great long distance rides

If you're up for a ride of more than 60 miles through some of the lower peninsula's wildest country, you'll love the long trails which end at the Mackinac Straits.

The North Central State Trail runs 62 miles from Gaylord to Mackinaw City, while the 72-mile North Eastern State Trail extends from Alpena to Cheboygan. A shorter route is the 35-mile stretch from Petoskey to the Straits.

In addition to the scenery and wildlife opportunities, these are the longest trails in Northern Michigan, all possible for experienced riders to do in a single day, albeit a long one...

Don't Miss:

- Tunnel of Trees
- Mackinac Island
- Petoskey to Mackinaw City
- Gaylord to Mackinaw City
- Alpena to Cheboygan
- Coast to Coast

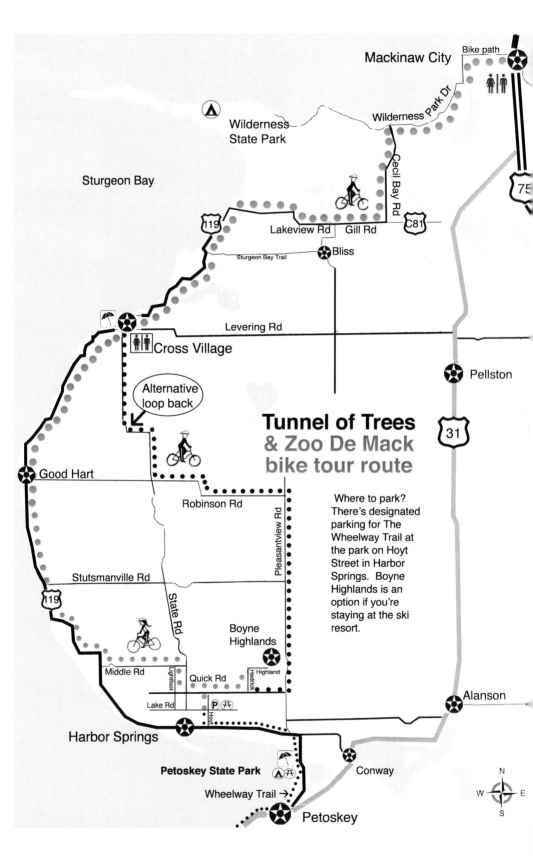

The Tunnel of Trees to Mackinaw City

Distance: 51 miles, one-way
Bike recommendation: Road bike or hybrid
Essentials: Fluorescent jersey, sunscreen, tool & tire kit, 2 water bottles, phone, raingear, energy foods
Traffic: Light to medium
Difficulty: Semi-tough because of distance & a few hills

The Tunnel of Trees route along US-119 from Harbor Springs to Mackinaw City is draped with superlatives from travel writers the world over, not to mention carpets of trilliums in bloom beneath its leafy bower every spring.

Like the ride around Torch Lake, you can either go it alone or hook up with thousands of other cyclists for the annual **Zoo-de-Mack** tour.

This quiet route is blessed with little traffic as you roll through the farmlands north of Harbor Springs. The fields morph into woodlands and a series of rolling hills along the Lake Michigan shoreline. The branches of overhanging limbs form the famed "tunnel of trees" -- a living cathedral which offers a soulful ride spring-through-fall.

After passing through Good Hart and Cross Village, you cycle on through Wilderness State Park and finish with spectacular views of the Mackinac Bridge.

CROOKED TREE

A good place to park in Harbor Springs is at The Wheelway Trailhead at the corner of Hoyt and Lake streets. It's the designated parking spot for the trail. You'll wend your way to the northwest to hit US-119. Also pictured on the map is the route from **Boyne Highlands** ski resort, located northeast of town.

About 18-20 miles along the route you'll find the **Good Hart General Store**, established in 1934, which offers refreshments and pot pies for weary riders. Perhaps you'll spot rocker Bob

Seger browsing the racks -- he's got a home nearby.

A few miles up the road you'll find the historic treasure of Cross Village. It was here in the 1670s that French Jesuit explorer Father Jacques Marquette planted a huge white cross on a dune overlooking Lake Michigan. To the hundreds of Ottawa and Chippewa Indians living in the area, the site became known as Wau-gaw-naw-ke-ze, or "Land of the Cross" and became the site of an annual gathering of many tribal bands.

To the French the village was known as L'Arbre Croche. Others called it Crooked Tree. Today, many members of the Little Traverse Band of Odawa Indians still live in the area.

LEGS INN

Whatever you do, be sure to stop at **Legs Inn**, one of the most unusual dining destinations in the Midwest.

The Inn was established by Stanley Smolak, a Polish immigrant who fled his native land in 1912 to avoid being drafted in the lead-up to World War I.

Smolak worked in the auto factories of Detroit and Chicago for a time, but settled in Cross Village in 1921 with his bride, Eleanor. They fell in love with the town and its Indian residents. Smolak soon grew enraptured with the twisting, sinuous forms of tree branches, driftwood and roots in the neighboring forest and along the beach.

Thus began one of the most singular creative endeavors in the history of Western art. Smolak's wooden tangles of roots, knots and limbs have no focal point or anthropomorphic meaning of any kind and are unparalleled in the art world. "Nature is the greatest sculptor - I am only helping to make the artistic objects more visible to the ordinary eye," he once said of his work.

You can still find examples of his sculpture amid the dusty relics on the walls of Legs Inn -- are they beautiful or simply bizarre? You decide.

Smolak began building the sprawling Inn in the late 1920s, adding an Indian curio shop. Throughout the '60s there used to be a teepee parked out front with a local character wearing a Great Plains Indian costume, posing for photos with kids.

Today, Legs Inn remains a lively destination throughout the summer, offering Polish specialties, outdoor dining and music.

The final stretch of the Zoo de Mack.

From Cross Village, you've got about 25 miles of easy riding through sandy forests to the Mighty Mac.

ALTERNATIVE ROUTE

If you only wish to bike the Tunnel of Trees and don't want to pedal all the way to Mackinaw City, you can head south on State Road from Cross Village. You'll hit Robinson Road and pedal east to Pleasantview Road back to Harbor Springs.

But be forewarned that State and Pleasantview roads tend to be busy with speeding traffic -- they are rural corridors for locals who don't care to take the twists and turns of Hwy 119. Pleasantview is also quite hilly.

The Zoo-de-Mack

Like company when you ride? More than 3,500 cyclists enjoy a virtual party on wheels each May, when the Zoo-De-Mack bike tour heads north from Boyne Highlands ski resort and up the coast through the Tunnel of Trees.

The tour got its start more than 25 years ago when Greg Draw-baugh and some friends from the Detroit area were up skiing at Boyne.

"We decided to take a trip to the U.P. and we drove up US-119 to get there," he recalled in an interview with *Northern Express Weekly*. "And I remember thinking, 'Boy, this is a beautiful road -- it would make a great bike trip.' So a few years later, the first mountain bikes came out on the market and we decided to make the ride."

Drawbaugh was 25 when he, his brother Doug, and a few friends from the Detroit area completed the first tour in 1989.

"There were eight of us riders the first year and we had a great time," he says. "The next year, we made up a little flyer and I think we had 88 people show up. One of the riders was Steve Kircher, whose family owned Boyne, and he encouraged us to keep the tour going. So the next year we had 250 riders, then 450 the year after that and it grew from there."

Today, what started as a word-of-mouth event has garnered a loyal following with more than 3,500 riders, many of whom return every year.

The tour includes refreshments at rest stops, sag wagon support and luggage transportation to Mackinac Island. Cyclists also enjoy a pre-ride party at the **Zoo Bar** at **Boyne Highlands** on Friday night, lunch at Legs Inn in Cross Village on Saturday, and post-ride parties with live music at **The Gatehouse, Pink Pony,** and **Horns** on Mackinac Island.

Riders are transported to and from the island on the Arnold Ferry line, with special extended hours from 10 p.m. to 2 a.m. Bike shuttles are available each way between Mackinaw City and Boyne Highlands (for a fee). Riders can either park their vehicles in town and catch a shuttle to Boyne Highlands on Friday night, or catch the shuttle back on Sunday. Some cycle the route in reverse.

The organization also offers a **Fall Frenzy Biketemberfest** from Boyne Highlands to Bay Harbor in September. Check the website for details on both tours.

Web: http://zoo-de-mack.com

Mackinac Island

Distance: 8 miles
Bike recommendation: All good
Essentials: Money for ice cream
Traffic: Horse-drawn carts
Difficulty: Easy

You roll into history whenever you put your feet to the pedals on Mackinac Island.

The island path is just 8 miles around its circumference and free of traffic , but oh, the sights you'll see... starting with the wigwam and the big white fort up on the bluff just outside of town.

From the 1600s through the early 1800s this island was considered one of the most strategically-important outposts on earth -- a Gibraltar in the New World which guarded the waterway to the fur trade beyond Lake Superior in Canada.

Furs from the Old Northwest made the fortunes of many French traders who sent their voyageurs west from Montreal. The fur trade also had a devastating effect on the Indians, who set about exterminating the beaver population -- and other tribes -- in pursuit of the white man's trade goods.

The British acquired the island in the late 1700s and built a small fort to protect themselves from the French and their Indian allies. The fort was acquired by the Americans in the 1783 Treaty of Paris, following the Revolution.

On a sleepy summer morning in July, 1812, the American garrison was surprised by a sneak attack from the unprotected rear of the fort. With their cannon trained on the waters of the Strait, the last thing the Americans expected was an attack by the British and their Indian allies from nearby St. Joseph Island, especially since they were unaware that war had been declared between the U.S. and Britain. Heavily outnumbered, they gave up without a shot.

OH FUDGE...

Mackinac Island is more of an experience than a cycling destination. You can rent bikes at the dock from a number of venues (consider a "bicycle built for two" to get in the 1890s spirit), or bring your own on the frequent ferries from Mackinaw City and

St. Ignace.

In town you'll find a glut of fudge, t-shirt and gift shops along with plenty of taverns and dining spots. Victorian inns line the streets in and out of town, offering pricey accommodations (cheap but chintzy digs are available in Mackinaw City on the mainland).

Of course, no visit is complete without a stop by the **Grand Hotel**, built in 1887 and boasting the "longest front porch in the world." The hotel is still considered one of the top-10 in the world, along with the likes of the Copacabana in Rio and Raffles in Singapore. It also offers budget room rates for those riding in the Zoo-de-Mack tour, including a superb breakfast buffet -- but reserve at least 6 months in advance because these rooms sell out early.

It's an easy ride around the island with only the wind to impede you. As you ride, consider that this island was once thought to be

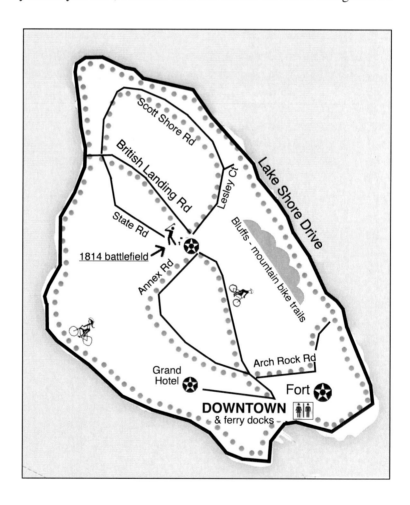

the home of Gitche Manito, the "Great Spirit" of the Ojibwe. Their chiefs gathered here for hundreds of years in tribal councils.

If mountain biking is your thing, you'll enjoy a tangle of rough trails on the bluffs along the eastern side of the island, some of which will perch you along cliffs that rise a couple hundred feet above the shoreline. People can and do fly off these bluffs to their deaths, so go easy...

A RIDE THROUGH HISTORY

For an offbeat ride, consider the route down the middle of the island. At the site of what is now the Wawashkamo Golf Club, you'll find an old battlefield where American troops launched a counter-attack against the British in 1814.

This is a lesser-known battle, but worth recounting. In late July, 1814, an American fleet of five gunboats and brigs left Detroit with 700 men to retake the island.

Unfortunately, they found that the British had built a new block-house above the town, the present-day Fort George, which was unreachable by cannon fire. Most of the casualties in the bombardment were veggies in the Brits' garden.

Hampered by fog, the American fleet circled to the north end of the island, returning a week later to bombard the woods in the hope of driving away any Indian warriors. Having lost the element of surprise, they stormed ashore only to be met by withering gunfire and cannonades from the British and their Indian allies as they crossed a field at the top of the island. Defeated, the Americans withdrew with their second in command shot to death.

Soon thereafter, the War of 1812 ended and the Brits returned the island. Today, few tourists visit this battlefield because it's something of a hike, but you, being the lucky cyclist, can pause to reflect here on the folly of war.

Also of note, the nine-hole Wawashkamo course is said to be the oldest continuously-played golf course in Michigan, established in 1898 by, who else? A native Scotsman named Alex Smith.

Overall, Mackinac Island is a gentle riding experience unless you're there for the mountain biking. Whatever you do, be sure to bring some fudge home for family and friends.

Web: http://www.mackinacisland.org

Petoskey to the Straits

Distance: 35 miles
Bike recommendation: Mountain bike or hybrid
Essentials: tools & tire kit, pump, sunscreen, first aid kit, phone, rain gear, 2 water bottles, energy foods
Traffic: None
Difficulty: Tough, because of distance on unimproved dirt trail

Quaffing a pint or two of locally-brewed beer at trail's end has become a ritual for me when riding the long, forested routes to the Straits. My favorite is Cheboygan Lighthouse Ale -- the ideal remedy for aching gluts, a sore bum, and the feeling that you've been beaten over the head with a whitefish after riding all day.

Indeed, your legs are likely to be aching at the end of the 28-mile Northwestern State Trail from Alanson to Mackinaw City, which is literally rough around the edges since it's an unimproved dirt pathway mixed with a tad of gravel from the former railway corridor. There's a lot more resistance on the spongy dirt of this path than you'll find on the limestone-paved routes to the Straits from Gaylord or Alpena, so it feels more like a 40 mile ride, and one on a mountain bike at that.

Ideally, you'll also want to include the new 7-mile stretch of paved trail from Petoskey to Alanson (see page 91) to give you a total 35-mile ride to the Straits. From Alanson it's a straight shot north on the dirt path to Mackinaw City, passing through Brutus, Pellston, Levering and forested areas further north.

As noted on page 93, a must-visit along this trail is the State Fish Hatchery Visitor Center at Oden about six miles north of Petoskey. Once you reach Alanson, ride down quiet Milton Street on the west side of town to pick up the trail paralleling US 31.

There's not much scenery on the southern half of the trail but you'll find some pleasant dining stops along the way. Check out the **Camp Deli** in Brutus for an 'Up North' experience; the rustic lodge-style diner is cram full of enough stuffed wildlife and huntin' memorabilia to warm the cockles of Ted Nugent's heart. Recommended: the hearty helping of redskin home fries.

The trail runs just 30 yards west of the buzz of traffic along US 31

The trail beyond Levering.

for two-thirds of its route and once you hit the dreary, windswept half-mile alongside Pellston Airport you may wonder what the heck you're doing here. Take heart, because just before Levering, the road veers away from 31, passing through miles of tamarack swamps and forest all the way to the Straits. This lonely stretch looks like a great place to spot a bear, deer or other wildlife.

Riders from the Top of Michigan Trails Council report good cycling on hybrid bikes along this trail, but in early May when the route was still squishy from spring rains, I was happy I opted for a mountain bike.

The final stretch into Mackinaw City offers a long, gradual downhill. Just past the wind turbines outside of town your heart will lift at the sight of a paved bike path that takes you all the way to the DNR Trailhead in the heart of the Mack.

With its barn-like budget motels, feeding-trough restaurants and souvenir stores packed with rubber tomahawks, family-friendly Mackinaw City is not what you'd call a 'classy' destination. For that you have to head to Mackinac Island and its pricey inns.

But for a cheap place to crash, you can't beat it, with motel rooms starting at $40. Check out the **Keyhole Bar & Grill** for authentic 'local' atmosphere, or **Audie's** restaurant if you're up for a hearty, family-style meal.

HEADING BACK

If you're up for a longer ride, the next day you can cycle the Tunnel of Trees route back to Petoskey, heading down US 119 (see page 101). Otherwise your options are spotting a car, taking the bus, or riding back the way you came. It took me exactly 4 hours to ride both ways from Bayfront Park in Petoskey to the Mack and back, cycling at a moderate pace with rests and a stop for breakfast.

The Top of Michigan Trails Council reports that there are plans to "eventually" pave the remainder of the route with crushed limestone. But for now, rejoice; this is your chance to ride one of the last unimproved long distance trails in Michigan.

Gaylord to Mackinaw City

Distance: 62 miles
Bike recommendation: hybrid bike
Essentials: Full tool & tire repair kit, raingear, phone, sunscreen, first aid kit, 2 water bottles, energy foods, rain gear
Traffic: None
Difficulty: Tough, because of distance

This sure seems like a good place to run into a bear, you think as you roll through the forest north of Vanderbilt. The North Central State Trail from Gaylord to Mackinaw City skirts the Pigeon River Forest and the trees are thick as a jungle on either side of the path, which runs like an arrow through the green.

Ernest Hemingway called this country "wild as the devil" when he camped on the Black River for several weeks in 1910 as a teenager with a band of chums. They spent their time catching trout and young Ernie had his own encounter with a black bear. Un-

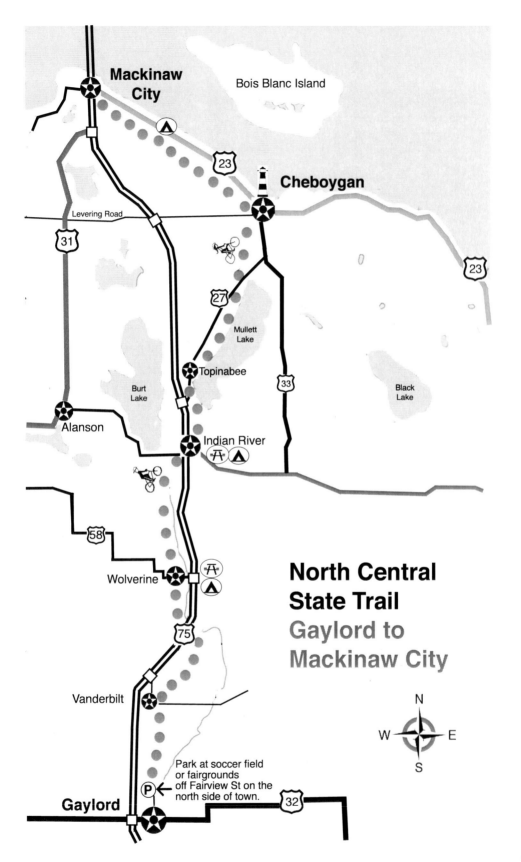

Mackinaw City

Bois Blanc Island

23

Cheboygan

Levering Road

31

23

27

Mullett Lake

Topinabee

Burt Lake

33

Black Lake

Alanson

Indian River

58

Wolverine

75

North Central State Trail
Gaylord to
Mackinaw City

N
W E
S

Vanderbilt

Park at soccer field or fairgrounds off Fairview St on the north side of town.

P

Gaylord

32

doubtably, he got some of the inspiration and material for his Nick Adams stories from the deep forest that stretches on either side of the bike path.

It's not quite the wilderness that it was back then, but it's as close to the real thing as anyplace you'll find in the lower peninsula, adding a roughing-it thrill to your ride. And although I was disappointed not to see a bear or one of the forest's many elk, a fat porcupine waggled his tail as I rolled past.

The 62-mile trail opened in the fall of 2007, wending its way through the forest and along the Sturgeon River and Mullett Lake.

Paved with crushed limestone and about 10 feet wide, the sparkling white trail is smooth and fast -- ideal for mountain bikes or hybrid cycles (no skinny tire bikes need apply, unless you're up for a wobbly, white-knuckle ride). In the winter, the trail becomes a pathway for snowmobiles.

The Top of Michigan Trails Council boasts that the route is "one of the premier cycling trails in the Midwest," and any weekend rider is sure to become a swift believer.

A TWO-DAY RIDE

The trailhead is located a mile north of Gaylord at the soccer field on Fairview Road, just off Old M-27. You can park overnight at the field alongside the cars of other riders. You can fuel up for the ride at the Bavarian-styled **Sugar Bowl** restaurant in town for breakfast or lunch, or enjoy dinner at the sprawling **Big Buck Brewery & Steakhouse.**

The seven-mile ride to Vanderbilt is surprisingly fast due to the fact that it's a gradual downhill all the way to the Straits. Before you know it, you're in Wolverine, another 10 miles or so further on.

Wolverine is a tiny burg, but has the distinction of having been the site of a training camp for the Northern Michigan Regional Militia back in the mid to late '90s. Back in the militia's heyday, reporters from around the world stopped by to grab footage and photos of camo-clad weekend warriors.

Wolverine also has a nice rustic campground and serves as an ideal put-in site for paddling the Sturgeon River, which is the fastest in Northern Michigan, dropping an average of 14 feet per mile.

An ideal paddle is from Wolverine to the town of Indian River, but expect to flip several times if you're in a kayak, and avoid the deadly log jams on the river bends at all costs; they tend to hold a sunken paddler underwater.

The stretch to Indian River offers the wildest country along the trail. But after crossing I-75, you're in for a shock: a **Burger King** greets you as you roll out of the forest at Indian River, and just across the way lies a **McDonald's**. Oh well, a little coffee and a sandwich can't hurt a weary rider. More discerning palates will find a smattering of locally-owned restaurants in town.

Farther on lie the tony cabins of Topinabee and then 15 miles of Mullett Lake's shoreline where the trail is at its manicured best. If you wish, you can take a splash at the park in your cycling shorts.

After Mullett Lake, the trail joins a bike path connecting Cheboygan with Mackinaw City. The 16-mile route paralleling the highway is through a tunnel of trees.

AT THE STRAITS

Chances are you'll be a bit wiped out by the time you catch sight of the **Mackinac Bridge**. Don't despair: there are numerous restaurants in town, and a park at the Straits offers a fine view of the bridge.

Completed in 1959, the Mighty Mac is five miles long, making it the fifth longest suspension bridge in the world and the longest of its kind in the western hemisphere. There are 42,000 miles of wire in the main cables, weighing in at 11,840 tons. It packs 931,000 tons of concrete and nearly 6 million rivets and bolts.

The Straits was the crossing preferred by the Ojibwe, the Ottawa, and the French voyageurs back when the fur trade passed through here in the 1600s and 1700s.

Today, you'll see freighters from around the world passing through from Chicago, Gary and Milwaukee, but the high winds blowing between Lakes Michigan and Huron can be treacherous: In 1989 a woman driving a tiny Yugo was blown right over the rail of the bridge -- a 200 foot drop to her death.

Mackinaw City also offers dozens of motels with budget rates and is the gateway to Mackinac Island. Multiple ferries leave every hour for the car-free island, which is very bike-friendly with an 8-mile perimeter trail. Be forewarned, however, that room rates are several times that of Mackinaw City, but then, so is the charm of staying in a grand old Victorian hotel and there's a great party scene every night at the island's many bars.

If camping is your thing, you can find a berth at **Mackinaw Mill Creek Camping** about three miles east of town on the way to Cheboygan. You're likely to feel like an odd duck here, however, since it's a big family scene.

If you don't care to ride back the next day, you can catch an Indian Trails bus which has regular service between Mackinaw City and Gaylord. The company's website claims that bikes must be packed in a bag or crated, but perhaps they'll give you a break if you call ahead.

BE PREPARED

Those who plan to ride the trail are advised to be prepared for any situation with a full tool kit, patches, pump, and possibly a spare tire as there are no bike shops for 30 miles around. You're in a self-rescue situation if you have a chain break or a sidewall blowout on your tire.

That's exactly what happened to me while riding south on the way back to Gaylord. There's nothing worse than a sidewall flat (in which the tire itself rips), since it can't be fixed with duct tape, and replacing the tube will simply result in another blow-out in a matter of minutes. Some claim that sidewall blowouts can be fixed by tucking a sheet of cardboard between the tube and the ripped tire. Bike shops also sell sidewall blowout patches, but they tend to be hard to find.

Unfortunately, there are no bike shops in Cheboygan -- the nearest cycle shop is 30 miles away in Petoskey. But Cheboygan has a hugemongous **K-Mart**, which sells bike tires reinforced with Kevlar.

The ride south back to Gaylord is tougher than the way north, requiring an easier gear. Reason? Mackinaw City is 590 feet above sea level, but Gaylord is at 1,349 feet elevation. That means you climb 759 feet on the way back, with most of that elevation being when you're dead tired on the last stretch between Wolverine and Gaylord.

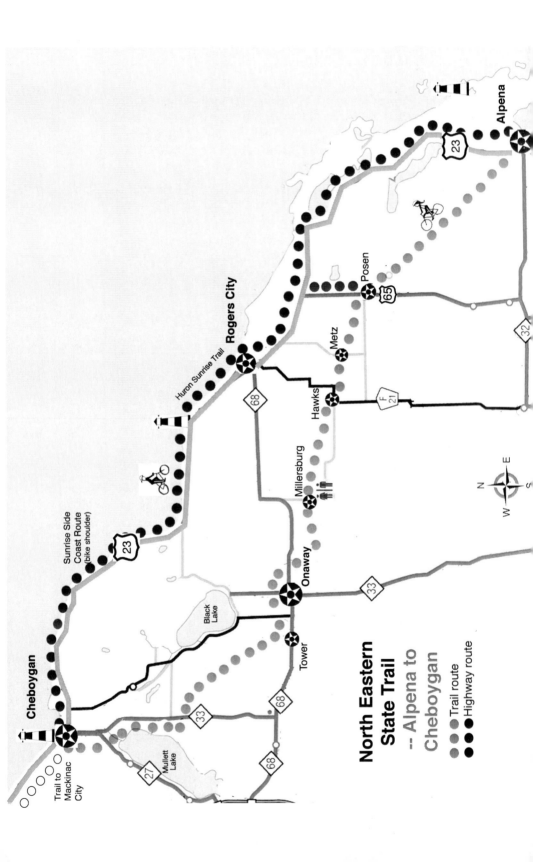

North Eastern State Trail
-- Alpena to Cheboygan

Legend:
- Trail route
- Highway route

Cheboygan

Trail to Mackinac City

Mullett Lake

27

68

68

33

Tower

68

Black Lake

Onaway

33

23

Sunrise Side Coast Route (bike shoulder)

Huron Sunrise Trail

Rogers City

68

Millersburg

Hawks

F 21

Metz

Posen

65

32

23

Alpena

N
W E
S

But somehow you make it, waving to fellow cyclists on the way back. You've rolled through half a dozen towns and some of Northern Michigan's most scenic forests -- a fine weekend adventure on one of the North's finest trails. This is one trail you don't want to miss if you love cycling.

For more information on the trail, check out the Top of Michigan Trails Council website at **www.trailscouncil.org.** The site includes a map and notes on each stretch of the trail along the route.

Alpena to Cheboygan

Distance: 72 miles
Bike recommendation: Hybrid or Mountain Bike
Essentials: Full tool & tire repair kit, sunscreen, phone, rain gear, first aid kit, energy foods, 2 water bottles
Traffic: None
Difficulty: Tough, because of distance

Two words of advice for those planning to ride the new North Eastern State Trail from Alpena to Cheboygan: Be prepared.

The old Boy Scout motto is apt for this 72-mile trail through some of the wildest country in the lower peninsula. Suffer a breakdown along this lonely path and you could find yourself walking 10 miles or more to the nearest town.

The new trail opened in 2011 as a collaboration between the Top of Michigan Trails Council, the DNR, MDOT and communities along the route. Paved with a 10-foot-wide surface of crushed limestone mixed with railroad ballast, the trail is open to snowmobiles in the winter and cyclists, walkers and horses from spring through fall.

RIDING NORTH

You can start at either end of the trail, but my wife and I elected to ride north from Alpena on a sunny day in early May, with a southern wind giving us an extra push.

There are several budget motels in Alpena to choose from, but the town has an appalling lack of restaurants compared to Michi-

WELCOME TO ONAWAY

1. TOM'S IGA
2. ONAWAY BAR
3. LYON'S MOTEL
4. ONAWAY MOTEL
5. NORTHLAND BAR
6. PORTER'S SURVEY
7. KAMMIES
8. MARATHON STATION
9. SHE
10. VANCE'S 76 STATION
11. SC
12. NORTHERN DI
13. CARTER'S FOOD
14.
15. SNOWMOBILE PARTS
16. VILLAGE
17. METROPOLE
18. DENNY'S
19. CIT
20.

LOCAL
INFO
↓

TAKE ONE

A sign worth 1,000 words...

gan's west coast. We lucked upon the **Olde Owl Tavern & Grille** downtown which offered a good carbo-loading meal of pasta and the cozy atmosphere of a hometown hangout. (Note: The Alpena Chamber of Commerce strongly disagrees with this assessment, stating there are dozens of restaurants in town, but they seem to be chiefly along the lines of Dairy Queen and McDonald's.)

There's a parking lot at the **Alpena Events Complex** on the north side of town where you can leave your car overnight. We got permission to leave our car at the giant truck stop on US 23 where it would be well lit at night.

Much of the trail runs straight as a yardstick. You roll through cedar swamps, forests and farmlands along the abandoned rail bed of the old Detroit & Mackinaw Railway line.

Once known as the "Turtle Line," this route operated between Bay City and Cheboygan from 1894-1992. It was built to transport the green gold of Michigan's forests to the lumber market downstate.

The lumberjacks of the late 1800s left behind massive brush piles that fed hell-roaring fires in 1908 and 1911. The fires generated flames up to 300 feet high and winds of hurricane force, killing hundreds of people and leaving dozens of towns burned to ashes.

A poignant story is that of a trainload packed with women and children who fled the village of Metz in October, 1908. Two miles out of town stacks of flaming hemlock bark and cedar posts lined each side of the tracks at a lumber crossing. The desperate engineer attempted to smash through, but the rails were so warped by the heat that the train derailed in the midst of a firestorm, leaving an open car full of screaming people -- 16 were cooked in their skins and dozens of others suffered horrible burns. A fireman on the train jumped into the tender's water tank and was boiled alive. And all this with the deadly winter coming on...

READY FOR ANYTHING

Today, much of the route is still as lonely as when the lumberjacks left it more than 100 years ago. You see lots of deer along the way, and we also spotted a porcupine, grouse and a snake, but alas, no bear, of which there must be plenty.

Some of the towns you pass, such as Posen, Hawks and Tower, aren't much more than crossroads. We felt lucky to snag an ice cream cone at a gas station in Hawks, which -- along with our gorp and granola bars -- served as lunch. There are restaurants in Onaway and Millersburg, but with 72 miles of trail riding to master, we were more inclined to keep rolling.

In early May the trail was squishy in spots as the result of heavy rains that spring. Even on our hybrid bikes there were soggy sections where it felt like we were riding on flat tires for several miles. A representative of the Top of Michigan Trails Council says, however, that she had no problem riding a skinny-tired bike the length of the trail in August when the surface is as hard as asphalt. So

You can't get lost on the way to Cheboygan...

draw your own conclusions based on the wetness of the season.

But in our case, riding in early May after a particularly wet spring, it was no hell-for-leather dash. Considering the mushy sections of this track and rest stops, we were lucky to average about 10 mph.

Also, as noted above, be ready for anything. You should have the ability and tools to fix your bike in the event of a breakdown or multiple flat tires. The closest bike shop may be 35 or more miles away. Otherwise, you can obtain some rudimentary bike parts, tubes and tires at the **Kmart** in Cheboygan.

Other must-haves for this trail are a first aid kit, bug spray, energy foods, water, rain gear and sunscreen. (I neglected to take the last item and got burned to a crisp.)

On the plus side, there is digital phone coverage on the entire length of the trail, and if you do have an unfixable breakdown, you could probably call a cab in Alpena to come and pick you up at one of the villages along the route, at considerable expense, of course.

The Northeast Michigan Council of Governments offers an excellent "Road and Trail Bicycling Guide" that includes the North Eastern Trail as well as the US 23 Sunrise Side Coastal Highway Heritage Route along Lake Huron. This detailed map is invaluable for finding scenic locations and for plotting alternative routes. You can order your map/guide or download a PDF at **www.us23heritageroute.org**

COMPARING ROUTES

The relatively new trail from Alpena to Cheboygan begs comparison to the 62-mile North Central State Trail that runs from Gaylord to Mackinaw City.

While the trail from Gaylord to Mackinaw City may be the more scenic of the two and 10 miles shorter, chances are if you've conquered one route, you'll surely want to ride the other.

By late afternoon, you roll past the north shore of Mullet Lake and into Cheboygan, sore in the bum and ready for a beer, a hearty dinner and a comfy motel bed.

How to get back? Easy. Indian Trails offers a Sunday morning bus service from Cheboygan to Alpena. Their website posts some sticky rules requiring that bikes be packaged in bags or crates, so call ahead to see if they'll give you a break.

Or, simply ride the 78 miles back down US 23 along Lake Huron. There's a bike lane on the shoulder of the road and virtually no traffic on Sunday morning. You can pick up the **Huron Sunrise Trail** at the 40 Mile Point Lighthouse and roll through PH Hoeft State Park for 11 car-free miles into Rogers City.

Although you may have the wind in your face and a few hills, riding the highway back to Alpena rewards you with views of Lake Huron, a lunch stop in Rogers City, and the satisfaction of having pedaled a total of 150 miles round-trip for the weekend.

Resources: www.us23heritageroute.org

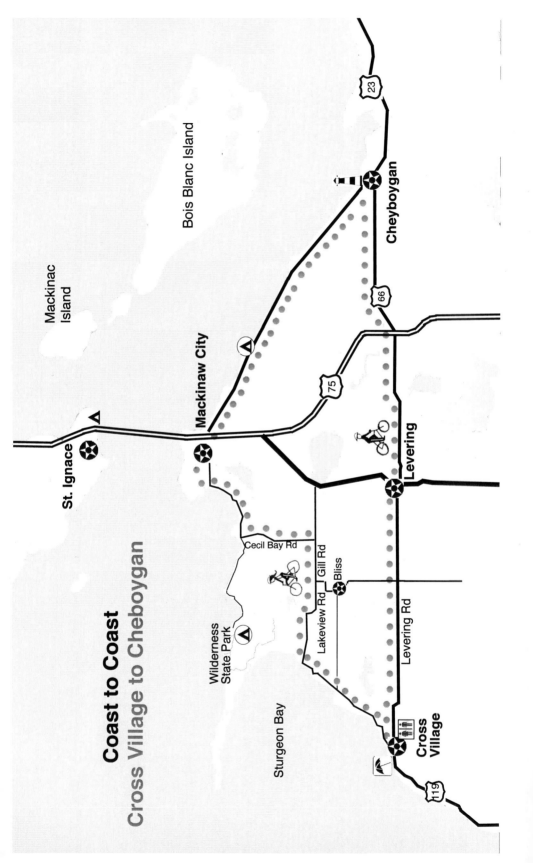

Coast to Coast

Cross Village to Cheboygan & Mackinaw City

Distance: About 70 miles
Bike recommendation: Road bike or hybrid
Essentials: Sunscreen, fluorescent jersey, tool & tire kit, phone, energy foods, 2 water bottles, rain gear
Traffic: Light to medium (along Levering Road)
Difficulty: Tough, because of distance, hills

This route gives you bragging rights for having biked all the way across the state from Lake Michigan to Lake Huron, albeit fudging a bit by riding the narrow 'tip of the mitt.'

The route rambles through the three crowning communities of the northern lower peninsula, each of which has its own sense of character.

Cyclists have been riding this cross-state trifecta as far back as the 1960s; in 1977 it was recommended as a touring route in a cycling guide issued by the Department of Natural Resources.

Starting in Cross Village you head east on Levering Road, straight as an arrow all the way across the state to Cheboygan. It's a narrow road and a bit of a roller coaster with plenty of hills along the way as you roll through farm country and forests.

Levering Road is also a main crossroads for traffic heading east and west. If it feels a bit too much, you can try riding Robinson Road a few miles to the south, which will take you to Pellston.

Midway across the state, you'll pass through the tiny burg of Levering, a legacy of the lumber era which appears to be on its way to ghost town status. Levering usually only makes the news when something goes wrong: In 1992, a convict serving up to 20 years on armed robbery escaped from a minimum security prison and went on a rampage through Northern Michigan, killing two men at a home in town before being captured in the Ludington area.

If you need to refuel, Levering is a good place to snack-up since it's nearly 30 miles across the state and this is the only town along the route.

Like Levering, Cheboygan has also seen better days, but the town is at its best along the riverfront where it maintains a maritime character. Be sure to stop at the **Crib lighthouse** at the junction of the Cheboygan River which stands sentinel to hundreds of freighters up to 1,000 feet long passing by through the shipping season, bound to ports around the world. There are several maritime-themed restaurants in town, including **The Boathouse** and **Pier 33** on the river which are popular with locals and tourists alike.

TO THE STRAITS

From Cheboygan, you have the luxury of riding for 16 miles along the relatively new bike path to Mackinaw City which parallels US 23. Along the way you'll pass the **Historic Mill Creek Discovery Park** offering zip line fun and a glimpse at the region's lumbering history.

Mackinaw City has its own charms, or lack thereof, as mentioned in other chapters on the routes to the Straits. Try the **Keyhole Bar & Grill** or **Audie's Restaurant** to sample the traditional side of the Straits.

Three hundred years ago, Mackinaw City was the site of a trading post and palisade fort that exchanged furs trapped by the Indians from throughout the Mississippi River Valley and Old Northwest for the pots, knives, axes and muskets of Europe. Initially an outpost of the French, the fort changed hands to the British in 1761 as an outcome of the French and Indian War.

The Brits' trading policies proved to be unpopular, however. It was here in 1763 that a band of Ottawa and Ojibwe warriors stormed the fort during a lacrosse game. An Indian lobbed the ball over the fence 'by accident' and when the British opened the gates the warriors streamed in with weapons hidden under the cloaks of their women. Most of the British were massacred as French traders and voyageurs looked on. **Fort Michilimackinac** was reconstructed in the 1960s just west of the Mackinac Bridge and remains a popular theme park for historical re-enactments.

From the DNR Trailhead behind Mackinaw Crossings you'll roll southwest along the town's new bike path until you come to Trails End Road heading right toward Wilderness State Park. Thereafter, you follow the same route used by the annual Zoo de Mack bike tour down along the sand hills of the coast to Cross Village.

Here of course, you'll want to claim your beer or a hearty helping of Polish cuisine at **Legs Inn**, the quirky folk art bar-restaurant described in greater detail on page 102.

Overall, this route feels like a good fit for the touring cyclist who's interested in exploring the character of the Straits, or if you're just up for some endurance training and want to rock the route down Levering Road.

Rest stop buddy - Carp Lake.

Big Tire Options
Some Choice Mountain Bike Trails

I ride a mountain bike almost every day for eight months of the year. But that's because I live in residential Traverse City where the streets tend to be pitted, cracked and potholed and a bike equipped with balloon tires and shocks is the best way to commute across town.

There are literally thousands of miles of mountain bike trails in Northern Michigan and several of the routes listed in this book lend themselves to riding on fat tires, including the route from TC to Kalkaska (page 29), the Betsie Valley Trail from Beulah to

Thompsonville (61), Beaver Island (95), Mackinac Island (105), and the limestone & dirt trail routes from Gaylord, Alanson and Cheboygan to Mackinaw City (pages 109, 111 and 117).

Otherwise, mountain biking is a topic worthy of a book in and of itself. Check out the Michigan Mountain Biking Association, which lists trails and events at http://mmba.org .

That said, here are a few trail highlights in the region:

• **Arcadia Dunes Singletrack:** Located north of the Village of Arcadia off M-22 in northern Manistee County, this 10-mile loop trail was created in the late '00s via a partnership between the Grand Traverse Regional Land Conservancy and the International Mountain Biking Association.

The many twists and narrow passages through trees along the trail may be a bit tough on inexperienced cyclists and there are plans to widen the trail. If you wish to call it quits halfway through, you can find your way back to the trailhead via adjacent roads, but pack along an area map or a GPS system or you could find yourself wandering around for a bit.

There's also a 5-mile hiking trail which takes you to a sweeping overlook of Lake Michigan atop "Old Baldy."

• **Vasa Singletrack:** This 10-mile trail runs counterclockwise through the woods southeast of Traverse City. Much-loved by local mountain bikers, you're likely to have some company out here.

From Traverse City, head east on Hammond Road, following it as it curves south and turns into High Lake Road. Go left (east) on Supply Road and look for the trailhead sign about two miles up.

• **Hartwick Pines:** This 10,000-acre State Park outside of Grayling offers three single-track trails along what was once a series of old logging roads. Starting from the visitor's center you'll find the 3.5-mile Aspen Trail for beginners. The tough get going on the hills of the 5.2-mile Deer Run Trail and the appropriately-named 7.5-mile Weary Legs Trail.

Nearby is the **Hanson Hills Recreation Area** offering 18 miles of trails and four major bike races from March-September.

• **Black Mountain:** Take it to the edge at the Black Mountain Forest Recreation Area which offers more than 30 miles of trails for cycling and XC-skiing in Presque Ilse County, 11 miles north of Onaway.

Located in the area between Black Lake and Lake Huron, Black Mountain towers more than 1,000 feet above the countryside. The mini-mountain was created by the retreating glaciers of the last ice age.

There's abundant camping in the area, or you can stay at the woodsy Black Mountain Lodge, but be forewarned, you'll have plenty of mechanized company: the area also offers 60 miles of ORV trails for quads and dirt bikes and more than 80 miles of snowmobile trails.

• **Glacial Hills:** One of the hottest mountain biking destinations in the north is located just north of Bellaire in Antrim County where you'll find 20 miles of trails in the 763-acre Glacial Hills Natural Area. Plans are underway to add an additional 10 miles of trail this year.

The area is named after the varied terrain of hills, gullies and ridgeways left by retreating glaciers some 20,000 years ago. It's an easy ride out of town to the closest trailhead on Orchard Hill Road.

• **Gaylord Area:** After fueling up at the Sugar Bowl restaurant in downtown Gaylord you can pedal a mere four blocks to Aspen Park to enjoy 5 miles of single track looping through alpine scenery. You may even spot one of the 70 or so elk at the nearby Gaylord Elk View Park.

• **The Cadillac Pathway:** This 60-mile trail is located on Boon Road off US-131 in Wexford County. The heart of the trail system is 10 miles of single track running along a series of rolling hills. The DNR trail is maintained by local volunteers.

• **Manistee's Big M Trail:** Runs 38 miles between Cadillac and Wellston off M-55. Manistee is also working on a non-motorized trail system.

• **Your favorite ski resort:** Virtually every ski resort in Northern Michigan offers mountain bike races and trail options to get through the "shoulder seasons" of spring and fall in between prime golfing and skiing weather.

Boyne Mountain, for instance, offers 7 miles of "killer views, hills and turns" on a paved loop, with 32.5-mile network of dirt trails, carriage paths and single track.

Boyne Highlands in Harbor Springs offers a Bike Park accessed by its ski lifts with trails spread out over 4,000 acres.

Crystal Mountain in Benzie County hosts the Peak2Peak mountain bike race on its trail network in October; **Mount Holiday** in Traverse City packs a crowd with its Mud, Sweat and Beers bike races in May. The list goes on...

Looking Ahead

In 2012, Governor Rick Snyder set the machinery of government in motion to develop a new 599-mile trail across the length of Michigan. By another estimate, the actual length of the trail could be as long as 924 miles, once all of its twists and turns are taken into account. Whatever the case, it will be a doozy of a ride.

The governor has pitched a trail that would run from Detroit's Belle Isle to the Wisconsin border in the Upper Peninsula. The idea is to showcase the best of Michigan for cyclists, hikers, snowmobilers and other off-road adventurers.

The proposed route will connect existing trails along the east side of the state from Detroit to Midland and then make a beeline for the Straits, utilizing the North Central State Trail that runs from Gaylord to Mackinaw City. From there, it will follow the northern coast of the U.P. to Ironwood.

To complete the project, 81.5 miles of new trail will have to be constructed in the Lower Peninsula -- mostly in southeastern Michigan -- and 152 miles of trail will have to be built in the U.P., linking a patchwork of current trails.

Gov. Snyder said a 2010 snowmobile trip from Marquette to Escanaba inspired him to propose a trail that would span both peninsulas.

"We got about halfway and ran out of snow," he said in a *Detroit Free Press* article. "But until you're out there in the middle of winter, you just don't understand how wonderful it is. It's absolutely pristine."

Snyder noted that Michigan has a huge, mostly untapped potential for tourism via its trail network. The governor hopes to make Michigan the "Trail State."

In 2013, Gov. Snyder directed the Department of Natural Resources to reach out to Michigan communities, trail groups and the federal government to determine how to make the proposed trail a reality

If and when the cross-state trail comes to pass, Michigan will cer-

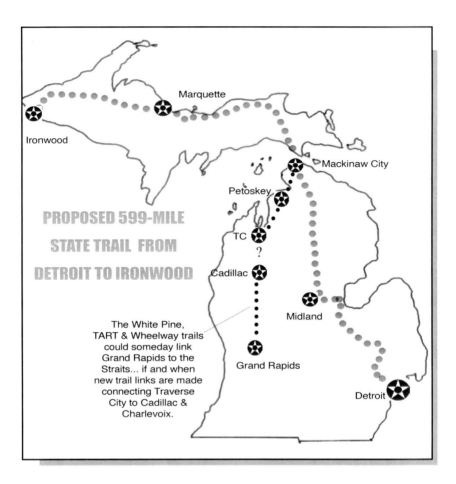

PROPOSED 599-MILE
STATE TRAIL FROM
DETROIT TO IRONWOOD

Marquette

Ironwood

Mackinaw City

Petoskey

TC

?

Cadillac

Midland

The White Pine,
TART & Wheelway trails
could someday link
Grand Rapids to the
Straits... if and when
new trail links are made
connecting Traverse
City to Cadillac &
Charlevoix.

Grand Rapids

Detroit

The cross-state trail from Detroit to Wisconsin would link the following existing trails and require the construction of new linking trails:

	Existing	Lower Peninsula
• Metro Parkway - Detroit Suburbs	**365**	**82**
• Paint Creek - Rochester/Lake Orion	Trail Miles	Miles Needed
• Polly Ann Trail - Holly		
• Southern Links Trail - Flint		Upper Peninsula
• Bangor/Bay Hampton Trails - Saginaw/Bay City		**152**
• Midland to Mackinac Boy Scout Trail		Miles Needed
• Northeastern State Trail - Mullet Lake/Cheboygan		
• North Central State Trail - Mackinaw City		

tainly reign as king of the nation's biking culture, with more trail miles than any other state -- the bona fide "Trail State," attracting millions of tourist dollars while advancing the lifestyle of visitors and residents.

For Northern Michigan, the most exciting development in the years ahead will be the construction of a trail from Traverse City to Elk Rapids and then on to Charlevoix.

That will make it possible to ride all the way from TC to the Mackinac Straits via The Wheelway Trail that runs through Petoskey -- a 100-mile route that will be a joy to ride.

Looking even further ahead, if and when a connector is built from Traverse City to Cadillac's White Pine Trail, it will be possible to cycle all the way from the Mackinac Straits to Grand Rapids and beyond. Someday, perhaps our grandchildren will know the freedom of cycling from Northern Michigan to Chicago, all on traffic-free bike paths.